WHY
IS THE
THIRD WORLD
POOR?

By Piero Gheddo

Translated by
Kathryn Sullivan

ORBIS BOOKS ● MARYKNOLL, NEW YORK

Originally published as *Terzo Mondo: Perche Povero?*
by Edizione P.I.M.E., Milan, Italy

Copyright © 1973 ORBIS BOOKS, Maryknoll, New York 10545
Manufactured in the United States of America
Library of Congress Catalog Card Number: 72-85793
ISBN 0-88344-757-6

CONTENTS

FOREWORD

"This nation can no more ignore poverty, hunger, and disease in other nations of the world than a man can ignore the suffering of his neighbors. The great challenge to Americans of this decade, be they private citizens or national leaders, is to work to improve the quality of life of our fellowmen at home and abroad."

These words, taken from President Nixon's message on foreign aid to Congress on April 21, 1971, make the best possible introduction to this book by Piero Gheddo. A veteran journalist of international renown and a missionary who has had prolonged personal contact with the "poverty, hunger, and disease" of underdeveloped nations, the author is well-qualified to illustrate the problems of the third world.[1]

One of the characteristics of the last decade was "the discovery of famine" in the world. We Americans, and other rich nations as well, became suddenly aware that famine exists and that it is very widespread through a large number of nations abroad—and that it also exists in our very own backyard, in the ghettos and slums of our own big cities, just a stone's throw away from our skyscrapers, opulent stores, and majestic buildings.

A flurry of activities followed this sad discovery. President Johnson declared war on poverty, countless organizations and programs were set up to fight poverty and to combat famine; billions of dollars from the government and private sectors were poured out to alleviate these conditions both at home and abroad. However, today, in the early seventies, poverty and famine are still with us—not only in our own country, but in most of the world as well. Almost two-thirds of mankind are condemned to live at a subhuman level and, unfortunately, too many of our people fail to realize how potentially explosive this situation is or are even slightly concerned about it.

The concept of a shrinking world—the global village, as it is called—has not yet been grasped by our people at large. Very few realize how we, by flaunting the highest standard of living ever achieved by mankind, contribute to the restlessness and misery of the poor nations of the third world and have reached almost the brink of a world revolution caused by famine and poverty. As President Nixon said so well in his recent message to Congress, the world order which insures peace and prosperity cannot be maintained "if two-thirds of the world's people see the richer one-third as indifferent to their needs and insensitive to their aspirations for a better life."

There are some very good reasons why we Americans cannot remain indifferent to this world situation. If we want to be consistent with the teachings of our Judaeo-Christian tradition, we must believe that we are "our brothers' keepers," that to help these billions of underprivileged people is not only a matter of charity, but rather of justice, and that it is also a matter of self-preservation and survival for our nation as well. As a people gifted with a great deal of practicality and common sense, our nation cannot fail to see that we must do something about this problem of poverty and famine in the third world.

The real problem, however, is that the average citizen of the United States is very poorly informed of the real situation in the third world; consequently, he has no great interest in alleviating it. This lack of knowledge and interest has been abundantly documented in recent times. The amount of foreign aid voted by Congress for the nations of the third world has been drastically reduced from year to year. We have descended from the second or third place among those nations contributing to help solve this problem, to the tenth place on a per-capita contribution of our gross national product to lower-income countries.

Our Peace Corps is faring badly. The Papal Volunteers for Latin America have been dissolved. Within our own Catholic Church, contributions to foreign missions in money and personnel are also decreasing. The whole trend is toward increased isolationism. This is really tragic because it is happening at the very moment when we have, by far, the largest gross national product in the world and the largest arsenal of ability and technical know-how to help solve the problems of the world.

Generally speaking, we have tended to oversimplify the whole matter. We have reduced it to an emotional affair and to a mere question of dollars. Now, when we realize that dollars alone are not enough, that the problems of the third world, despite our generous contributions, are growing worse each day and that anti-American feelings abroad are growing deeper and louder, we, as humans, are tempted to "throw in the sponge" and rid ourselves of the whole messy business, from Vietnam to foreign aid—and even to helping our foreign missions. This is a tremendous mistake!

There are numerous and complicated reasons for our past failures. First, there is the deep lack of knowledge of the very people whom we want to help. We have gratuitously assumed that other people are like we are and respond to the same stimuli as we do. We have forgotten that our United States is a country very unique in the world because it has been constituted mostly of people who have fled other highly civilized nations in search of freedom—and that love of freedom is at the very root of our nation. This is not so in other countries which have been accustomed for centuries to live under dictatorial regimes and which have completely different cultures, traditions, and mentality from our own.

We have gone ahead, lavishly distributing our dollars and failing to realize that most of our financial help, in too many countries, has only helped the rich become richer and the poor become poorer. We have pretended to impose our standard of life and our technological methods on people who have no interest in mechanics and who are still quite satisfied to plow their land with the same type of plow used four thousand years ago. However, a more serious mistake is that we have failed to concern ourselves with integral development. We have studied and written a great deal about socioeconomic development, technological development, agricultural development, industrial development and educational development; but we have never made a synthesis of all this and developed a real concern for the integral development of the nations of the third world. Without such development, which, besides his basic, human needs, embraces the soul and spirit of man, our efforts were doomed to failure from the very beginning. Only now do we begin to realize the whys and hows of these failures.

There is no doubt that if we want to really help solve these problems and achieve greater results from our contributions, we must begin with an in-depth study of the people we want to help, and adapt our dealings with them to suit their particular mentality and their needs. We must become aware that the development of the third world is an extremely complicated affair and that there is no immediate and easy solution. Some might think that these problems could be solved through greater generosity and justice on the part of the rich countries as well as greater financial help, fair trade treaties, the elimination of custom tariffs and of political pressures, etc. Essentially, all of this would help, but it would not be enough.

Even if all the rich countries of the world were to exercise perfect justice towards the poor—even if they contributed not 1 percent, but 10 percent of their riches—this would not mean that the underdeveloped nations would automatically set out on the road toward development. The reason is that development is not something that can be imported from abroad; it is a process which must be undertaken by means of *internal* force through education, the changing of mentality and pretechnical social structures, the acceptance of a common discipline of work, political maturity, the learning of modern techniques and, above all, the acquisition of the concept of the dignity of man. This is the real, integral development without which there can be no development at all.

It is along this line of thought that Piero Gheddo's contribution to the understanding of the problems of development is most significant. The author points out that the primary responsibility of development lies with the very countries which are technically underdeveloped. This does not mean that we can be relieved of the responsibility of helping them; on the contrary, we must adopt an enlightened policy that is oriented toward the true cause of underdevelopment. Hence, the title of the book, "Why is the Third World Poor?" It is of prime importance, in our concern for the third world, to understand well the deep causes of poverty among these people and to realize that it is not a question of some superficial, easily corrected, situation. This is an age-old situation with deep roots in the very cultures of the people.

Many within the last decade who were greatly enthused about solving these problems are today frustrated people and have already given up their efforts, or are tempted to do so. This is not uncommon and has happened even at the very highest levels. On April 30, 1946, the French government inaugurated a plan to develop their own overseas possessions, foreseeing the development of these lands into "modern and developed nations" within fifteen years. A few years later, in 1956, Belgium launched its thirty-year plan for the development of the Congo. Needless to say, all these plans are still very far from their goals.

It is important, therefore, to give up the illusion that the fight against famine is a simple matter that could be solved simply through money, commerce, loans, expertise, etc. Nor is it something that can be achieved within a few years—nor, probably, even within a few decades. It will be a long, uphill, hard-fought battle, requiring the maximum interest and involvement on the part of humanity for the next fifty years, at least.

Another important contribution of Gheddo's book is to present to the American public the fact that the long-term solution to the problems of the third world cannot be found either within the terms of the liberal-capitalists' theory of development, or the Marxist-communist theory. The author illustrates the spiritual and Christian vision of development as the very basis of social action, because without these guided principles animating our activities we are doomed to failure. It is a fact that even during this post-Vatican Council era and in spite of many papal documents on development, too many Christians have no concept of the practical consequences which derive from Christian inspiration in the social and political fields.

This is why too many Christians are leaning toward either the Marxist or the capitalist concept of development and virtually ignoring the Christian vision. Not only Europe, but even here in the States, we lack an in-depth study which might popularize the concept of development according to the Christian vision of man. It is therefore no surprise that many, especially among our younger generation, not finding guidance from their Church, look for it in other sources which are alien to our Christian concept of the world.

This book is intended not only to help every serious person to understand the problems of famine in the world but to help those who are directly involved in development work to better grasp the basic principles which should guide and inspire their activities.

Another purpose of the book is to help enlighten public opinion in support of our country's Foreign Aid Program. Apart from political views, the recent message of President Nixon to Congress is certainly a very enlightened program which fully deserves the country's support. Our President is planning to revamp the entire Foreign Aid Program by coordinating the work of some of the already existing agencies and establishing new agencies which would bring about the cooperation of the government officials and outstanding private citizens in the field of research on the key problems of development, loans, grants, and other types of financial assistance.

President Nixon has said: "Foreign policy is not a one-way street. It requires that other nations understand our problems and concerns, but it also requires that we understand theirs." It is doubtful whether our public opinion is enlightened enough to fully endorse this program. Unfortunately, in recent years, public opinion with regard to foreign aid has been so warped and ill-informed as to deserve what William S. Gaud, head of the Foreign Aid Agency in Washington, defined as a "retreat from responsibility." Perhaps it is not too much to hope that this book may help many to face their responsibility towards the poorer nations of the world.

This book should serve not only to encourage those who have already been personally involved in relieving the problems of the third world, but to inspire many others to join their ranks, so that our great country may lead the world in stimulating interest, concern, and valuable help to the poor of the world.

We applaud the Maryknoll Fathers for their initiative in translating and publishing this important contribution by Piero Gheddo. In doing so, this great foreign mission society fulfills its role in its effort to make the Church a vital force in solving the problems of the third world. The Church, in fact, must be a "leaven for a better world," and she has to give soul to the earthly and human realities. It is primarily within this context that Pope Paul calls the missionaries the "pioneers of material progress and cultural development."

In a recent article in *The Homiletic and Pastoral Review* I wrote:

"It is, first of all, by announcing Christ and by inviting all men to accept his message that the Church can give the world the new soul it needs; in turn, it will be from this new soul that will come profound transformations in the political, economic, and social life of the world. Then men will establish new interrelations which will assure the harmonious and integral development of all peoples."

—Reverend Nicholas Maestrini, PIME

---

1. "The third world" comprises that group of about eighty-eight underdeveloped nations, mostly in Asia, Africa, and Latin America, which are neither a part of the communist world, nor do they belong to the group of highly developed and technologically advanced nations of North America, Europe, and Japan. Our government, in its official documents, calls these nations "the lower-income countries," but this expression might also apply to the poorer nations of the communist world which constitute a group of their own and are practically beyond the reach of our influence. This is why we adopt the more universal expression of the "third world" to include all the lower-income countries in the free world outside the communist orbit.

INTRODUCTION

In December 1964 when I took part in the Food and Health Seminar held in Bombay under the auspices of the Catholics of India, experts in agricultural problems seemed somewhat discouraged. That great country, despite noteworthy efforts on the part of the government, had not yet succeeded in producing sufficient food for its nearly 500 million inhabitants. I recall, however, the words of optimism brought to this meeting by Cardinal Valerian Gracias. His undaunted hope in the future of India impressed the experts and was eventually proved to be justified. For today, though India's population far exceeds that of 1964, it can be said that, barring some unforeseen natural catastrophe, the country has passed the difficult point of its development and moved beyond the spectre of universal hunger.

There are many other problems in the world that may seem at first to have no solution; but they should be tackled and probed in depth. This is the significance of Piero Gheddo's book. For more than ten years he has been active in the war against hunger. He has done what he could to share with others his understanding of and his love for the people of the third world.

The message of this book is that faith in man, faith in the future of man and of all men must be sustained. Man is central to every form of development; nothing can be done without his collaboration. Goals are achieved only because men truly desire them. This fact has to be understood today. Otherwise man may stand, as it were, aloof from the struggle for development, by trusting totally in machines, in ideologies, in economic-financial plans. I have gone around the world several times, and speak from experience. I have been a participant in a hundred congresses on development. I have conferred with politicians, technicians, bankers. I have followed closely the progress of development in the third world. All the political failures I have seen can be reduced in the last analysis to the fact that in every one there has been little respect shown for man and no attempt made to vitalize the human community but only to introduce machinery and to make changes on the map.

I have seen countless "agrarian reforms," especially in Latin America, which produced results that were more negative than positive. Why? Because it had not been understood that the reform of farming should begin with the reform of man. This means the reform not only of the rich landowners but also of the poor worker in the field or factory. Therefore the most radical revolution, inspired by the best intentions, will change nothing, unless it succeeds in changing man's thinking. Examples in recent years do not fail to support this premise.

Piero Gheddo's work, inspired by a truly Christian and human spirit, seems to me to deal with specifics, and it is based on a profound understanding of conditions as they actually are in the third world. Whoever has studied the people of this world and lived with them for more than a few days or weeks cannot but agree with what the author has written. It goes without saying that the struggle for improving the lives of poor people is to be a long one, requiring perseverance, a firm, clear vision of what is to be done, and a deep commitment on the part of all. During my worldwide travels I have heard so many technicians and missionaries lament that there have been no responses to their efforts and proposals for development. But they also know that lights cannot be lit where wires and electric power are lacking. Man—any man—possesses gifts and powers that are almost infinite; however, the miracle of a man taking his first steps on the road to development cannot be expected to occur until both he and his community have been made aware of their latent capabilities.

There are other observations to be made on points that Piero Gheddo has developed too briefly in this volume. I love the earth. I work it. Even today, almost under the cupola of Saint Peter's,

I farm it as I have done all my life. I know the earth and the many treasures it contains. When I was involved in the study of land cultivation in the United States and then, for many years in the FAO (Food and Agriculture Organization), I was many times directly aware that development starts with agriculture, with work in the fields. For the underdeveloped world, the first requisite is to teach the farmer how to produce more and better food. Today this is done too rarely. Hundreds of millions of workers in the fields labor hard with little satisfaction. They feel excluded and frustrated. Few ever think of helping them to grow. Few ever reveal to them the greatness and nobility of their physical efforts in the fields. Yet, essentially, the future of their countries and of a great part of mankind depends on them. There will be no progress until the rural masses are freed.

Man is the maker of his own destiny, but on the condition that he is truly man: conscious of his dignity, his strength, and free from all oppression and exploitation; on the condition that he begin to rise even a little above the most abandoned of men. This is the great goal that the second decade of development proposes.

To be a pessimist is to be neither a man nor a Christian. This volume of my friend, Piero Gheddo, with his clear vision of the reality of the third world, is a stimulus to involve oneself in the challenge of our century: the alleviation of hunger and misery in the world. It only remains to wish that this book receives the widespread attention it deserves.

Luigi G. Ligutti
President of *Agrimissio*
Rome, Italy

TOWARD A CHRISTIAN VIEW OF DEVELOPMENT

1

The following was written by an Englishman, and what he says of his countrymen applies equally well to people in all developed countries:

> Development is imperiled by those who are trying to over-popularize it. This danger will not be a death due to neglect but to an excess of superficial knowledge. . . . Everyone is talking about development, but what is it in reality? One thing is certain: It has no single meaning. Development means something different to each one who speaks.[1]

WIDESPREAD CONFUSION ABOUT THE IDEA OF DEVELOPMENT

Interest in the underdeveloped countries of the third world is a very recent phenomenon. We clearly recall that ten years ago, when the UN launched The United Nations Development Decade, neither newspapers nor the general public were in the slightest degree interested in the UN's initiative. Today this attitude has changed, particularly among the youth, who were aroused not only to interested concern but also to dedicated action. Now, in England as everywhere, the question of development is in danger of death because of over-popularization and the absence of any clearly defined idea.

Following a first phase marked by incredulity ("But is it really true that people are dying of hunger?"), there was a second phase in which graphs, statistics, and tables were the dominant elements. This was the time when there was endless discussion about calories and proteins and the median per capita income, and when comparisons were made between the number of pounds of meat consumed by an American in one year and the few ounces that an Indian could afford.

Today the problem is not so much to show that hunger and want really do exist, or to point out the immense abyss separating rich and poor countries, but to find out how all this has come about and, above all, how can it be remedied. In a word, interest is not so much in underdevelopment per se, but in its root causes and the ways to counteract them—*development, yes; but what kind of development?*

It is useless to add that immediate needs and the discovery of the various kinds of underdevelopment that exist have led to amazing confusion about the meaning of the word among those who study or who are interested in the subject. It is easy to understand how this has happened. It is far easier to describe a phenomenon such as hunger than it is to discover its causes and to propose remedies; in addition, studies about development in the third world are still fragmentary and have not yet been brought to scientifically certain conclusions. It should also be added that, in this field as in any other, the different students and authors are influenced by their own particular vision of the world, of man, of history, and of the politico-economic theory in which they believe. This influence is all the more powerful because basic indices and data are still lacking so that there is a tendency to judge the third world on the basis of a preconceived theory rather than on concrete reality.

NOT ALL FORMS OF DEVELOPMENT ARE ACCEPTABLE

It is natural, therefore, that the general public, having as yet no clear ideas about development, are led to accept uncritically, with closed eyes as it were, whatever is written on the subject. Many declare that in a term like "development of the third world" (or "the struggle against underdevelopment") there can be no ideological differences, for all are unanimous in wanting progress, development, and justice. This is a simplistic view. It is true that everyone says they are in favor of development, but—again—what kind of development?

The races in South Africa cry to the four winds that their pattern of the separate development of races (which is another way of saying apartheid) ensures the rapid development of all. Probably many say this in good faith. But do they mean what *we* mean by justice and development? Evidently not. We must admit that theirs is a kind of justice and development that we do not accept. And there are many others interpretations that we find unacceptable. I am thinking now of justice and development as they are found in the Portuguese colonies. Without a doubt the vast majority of the Portuguese are convinced that their form of development is ideal. I am also thinking of justice in Russia under the Soviet regime—and development in Czechoslovakia under the Soviet heel.

To conclude: There are various concepts of development that may agree in certain aspects, but differ in others. These may be reduced to three categories. Two are materialistic in inspiration: economic liberalism and Marxism. The third is spiritual, inspired by the encyclical On the Development of Peoples (*Populorum Progressio*) and other documents of the Christian church, and by Christian authors (Lebret, Perroux, Barrère, Ward, McCormack, Clark, Albertini, Cosmao, Houtart, and of course, Teilhard de Chardin). This third understanding is called spiritual rather than Christian inasmuch as it is not derived exclusively from Christian thinking but from the thinking of all religions. Gandhi, for example, belongs in this category by virtue of his understanding of development in India.

It is extraordinary that four years after its publication, Development of Peoples has had so little influence on public opinion and Christian groups who are dedicated to the struggle against hunger. Today the encyclical is remembered as a cry of alarm over the insupportable situation of poor countries, yet the Christian concept of development presented in its pages has not been sufficiently studied or publicized. Consequently, even in Christian circles there has been *an amazingly confused idea of development* which certainly has not favored an enlightened and authentic dedication to the struggle against hunger.

MAN AND THE DRIVING FORCE OF DEVELOPMENT

What then is development? Let us begin our search for greater clarity by examining the concrete differences and similarities in the spiritual idea of development and those of materialistic inspiration, whether derived from capitalism or Marxism.

For those who believe in God, development is above all else man's response to a definite divine vocation:

> In the design of God, every man is called upon to develop and fulfill himself, for every life is a vocation (Dev. Ppls., 15). Endowed with intelligence and freedom, he is responsible for his fulfillment. . . . Each one remains, whatever be the influences affecting him, the principal agent of his own success or failure (*Ibid*). In the socioeconomic realm, too, the dignity and total vocation of the human person must be honored and advanced along with the welfare of society as a whole. For man is the source, the center, and the purpose of all socioeconomic life (Pastoral Constitution on the Church in the Modern World) (*Gaudium et Spes*, 63).

All creation has meaning only in man, who is the center of nature and the first author of his own transformation. Christianity sees nothing higher than man, except God his creator—not nature and far less technology, economics, ideology, political life, the state, and society, which should all be directed toward the growth and development of man.

Development, therefore, in the Christian concept, is seen first of all as man's answer to God, who calls upon man to develop himself and gives him the specific means to do so by making him a thinking creature and the ruler of creation. Only by beginning with man can the development of the whole society and of mankind be advanced and achieved: "What we hold important," affirms Development of Peoples quoting Father Lebret, "is man, each man and each group of men, and we even include the whole of humanity" (n. 14).

Here is the notable difference between the spiritual and the materialistic concept: The former holds that *man is the driving force behind development* (Josué de Castro has written, "Man's brain is the prime mover of development"). The latter, on the other hand, attributes development essentially to technical, economic, and struc-

tural causes. As for the mechanistic theory of classic economic liberalism, this holds that development is caused principally by the accumulation of capital understood as the increment of physical means of
production; that is, savings and investment, the multiplication of
mechanical and technical improvements. Marxism teaches that
development is the result of liberation from external oppression,
or, in other words, liberation from exploitation by the owner on
the business level, and from imperialism on the international level.

It is not always a question of fundamental differences; often it
is no more than a slightly greater stress on one element than on
another, with the risk of falsifying the whole perspective of development. For example, the spiritual and Marxist conceptions are not
mutually exclusive. The first stresses the fact that man is the author
of his own development; therefore the first thing to be done is to
awaken man, instruct him, enable him to work, give him an understanding of his rights and the opportunity to raise his standard of
living and so forth. The second affirms that *development depends on
the struggle against others* for liberation from an external oppression
that hinders man's growth. It is a different stress but an important
one.

The Christian concept does not exclude a struggle against oppression when this is necessary. But it does not agree that all failures
in development are caused by external oppression and hence where
there is no development there is necessarily oppression and exploitation. This is what Marxism holds, and by doing so, neatly divides
the national community and the international community into the
exploiters and the exploited.

There is also another concept, found in many forms. Like the
liberal concept it does not consider the human factor but holds
only a mechanistic view of society. It should be added that, in
regard to the third world, this way of thinking has become fairly
common, even among Christian authors. When an underdeveloped
country is being discussed—be it the Congo or the Sudan, Brazil
or Bolivia, India or Indonesia—the poverty in the country in question
is attributed to imperialism (American), to colonialism and neocolonialism, to commercial exploitation, to the injustices perpetrated
by the international market for raw materials, etc. It is as though
the internal cultural and sociological causes of underdevelopment
scarcely existed—at least no reference is made to them. To us, this

is a Marxist or communist analysis of the underdevelopment of the third world.

As will be shown later, the practical consequences of this fundamentally different position are of considerable importance. Here it need only be said that for the Christian for whom development is a human fact, the principal obstacles to development are to be found in insufficient human preparation and inadequate formation of the human factor. Thus underdevelopment in the last analysis could be defined as the cultural, psychological, and social failure to accept modern progress with all its exigencies.

Consequently the Christian claims that the main thrust toward the development of a people should be through education, through their human formation. In a word, the decisive factor is man and his formation in depth, because it is then man can do all the rest—change structures, produce the necessary capital, overthrow the oppressor, etc.

Archbishop Thiandum, of Dakar, said when addressing a French congress:

> I believe that I can say, without fear of error, that underdeveloped countries need education more than they need money or clothes. Financial help, no matter how valuable this may be, cannot be a substitute for a people's desire to win its place in the world's economic scene, for the skill and strength of its own sons. The primary purpose of technical help seems to me to be first of all, and above all, a work of education.[2]

This presentation of the problem differs vastly from capitalism and Marxism. Here the accent is placed on the human factor rather than on factors that have little value. If man is not formed he is not prepared to make use of these other factors.

MAN'S PRIMACY OVER ALL

What then is this development to which all men are called? The Pope defines it this way:

> . . . a development which is for each and all the transition from less human conditions to those which are more human (Dev. Ppls., 20).

More precisely, "less human" means hunger, oppressive social structures, injustice, illiteracy, and the like. Conversely, "more human" means the access of those in want to the possession of what they need, victory over social wrongs, the recognition of supreme values, faith in God, and "union in the charity of Christ" (Ibid., 21). Therefore, according to the Pope:

> Development cannot be limited to mere economic growth. In order to be authentic, it must be complete, that is, it has to promote the good of every man and of the whole man (n. 14).

Consequently it is necessary to establish a clear-cut scale of values in human progress. Development does not simply mean "to have more":

> But the acquiring of temporal goods can lead to greed, to the insatiable desire for more, and can make increased power a tempting objective. Individuals, families, and nations can be overcome by avarice, be they poor or rich, and all can fall victim to a stifling materialism (n. 18). To have is not the ultimate goal of nations or of men. . . . Both for nations and for individual men, avarice is the most evident form of moral underdevelopment (n. 19).

The revolutionary idea of Christianity is that of *man's primacy* over everything else, over his own society. In fact, society is meant to help man to realize his own powers and not vice versa. Man transcends society. This does not lead to absolute individualism (each one for himself and God for all), because man is social and cannot develop himself in isolation but only in relation to society. It means that socioeconomic development finds its full justification as a service to man, as an opportunity given to man to develop integrally all his potentialities, not only the physical and intellectual, but also the moral and spiritual.

Development means *"to have more in order to be more"* (Dev. Ppls., 6). Therefore, economic and social growth is for man's service and his moral and spiritual growth. "A man is more precious for what he is than for what he has" (Church in the Modern World, 35).

Here the differences between the spiritual and the material understandings of development are notable. For the Christian the "economy should be at the service of man" (Dev. Ppls., 26), because "economics and technology have no meaning except from man whom they should serve" (n. 34). In contrast, both the capitalist and communist systems place man at the service of the economy. He is no more than a specialized cog in the production machinery of the system. Granted, economic liberalism is not what it was in the days of Adam Smith and David Ricardo. It is also true that communism since Stalin has moved into "socialism with a human face" of which the Czechoslovakian spring gave some indication. But it cannot be denied that in both camps the dignity of man and the equality of all men is not recognized in practice. The absolute superiority of the fundamental rights of the human person are not admitted even in theory. Therefore man is denied any real opportunity of realizing himself as an end. We are not speaking even of those supernatural ends that transcend the human person.

This is the fundamental difference between the Christian and Marxist understandings of development: *the primacy of the person over all the rest*, the value of the single individual (man created in the image of God) and the fundamental rights of the human creature that must always be safeguarded. Don Girardi—in a book about dialogue with Marxism, which was praised by the Marxists themselves for its openness and understanding—states that "if Marxism wishes to overcome the importance given to the totality by means of an internal development" it must admit that "such development implies a deep change in the perspective regarding the naturalist and collectivist version current in Soviet communism and from which many have drawn their inspiration. This implies in the first place the recovery of the relatively autonomous and unconditional value of the person as the end and agent of his own history and, to that extent, the solid foundation of all values."[3]

In a letter addressed to the 38th Social Week of Italian Catholics (Salerno, September 24-29, 1966), Pope Paul wrote:

> An appropriate economic development presupposes a just concept of the human person, of man's preeminent value in his dignity and in his freedom, in his responsibility and in his place in society. Economic development can no longer draw its fundamental orientation from science and technology, nor from economics alone but should find it in the true understanding of man, the community, and history. This is to say that economic development has to be realized within the confines of the moral order. . . .

Since man is the center, the foundation, and the end of development, it follows that this can be realized only in a human way, that is, in a way that fully respects his sphere of personal freedom and dignity which is characterized by his inner and transcendental values.[4]

Capitalism and Marxism seek to accomplish the progress of society in its entirety. So it matters little if the individual is crushed in the machinery of production or in the worship of the state (*Ibid*). This is a form of development that the Christian does not consider development. For this reason it is necessary to avoid judging progress on the basis of economic and technical success. Nazi Germany was unquestionably a land economically and technically advanced, but it was certainly not developed in a Christian sense. The same holds true for South Africa, because of its racism, and all other countries where the people are crushed by various kinds of authoritarian regimes and by oppressive structures. The basic criterion of development is therefore the opportunity that the person has for self-fulfillment and integral self-development in a given society, and the progress this society is making toward achieving its goals. There are no totally developed countries and there never will be. *Any society, like any man, is always on the way to further development*. The important thing is that there be no structured obstacles, such as state racism or dictatorship, for example, to block the march forward.

THE TRAGIC ERRORS OF LIBERAL CAPITALISM

The development described in Development of Peoples applies not only to the individual man but to all men:

There can be no progress towards the complete development of man without the simultaneous development of all humanity in the spirit of solidarity (n. 43).

The reason for this is easy to understand. Man is a social being. He cannot develop in isolation, but must do so by contributing to the development of others, that is, he must act in universal solidarity within the limits of his own country and the whole human family.

Paul VI traces in the second part of the encyclical the direct line of the total development of all mankind, recalling the three duties of rich countries towards the impoverished ones:

> The duty of human *solidarity*—the aid that the rich nations must give to developing countries; . . . the duty of *social justice*—the rectification of inequitable trade relations between powerful nations and weak nations; . . . the duty of *universal charity*—the effort to bring about a world that is more human toward all men, where all will be able to give and receive, without one group making progress at the expense of the other (Dev. Ppls., 44).

In the actual state of the world today, everyone knows that these principles of development are not respected by rich countries—either capitalistic or communist—notwithstanding the first timid attempts at solidarity and international justice that have not succeeded in putting an end to present injustice. These are rooted in the past and have continued to the present day primarily through the fault of economic liberalism that considers

> . . . profit as the key motive for economic progress, competition as the supreme law of economics, and private ownership of the means of production as an absolute right that has no limits and carries no corresponding social obligation (Dev. Ppls., 26).

This denunciation in the encyclical labels "unchecked liberalism" as "the international imperialism of money" (*Ibid*).

Papal and conciliar documents contain many condemnations and negative evaluations of capitalism. These judgments are not based on the system considered in itself but bear on the concrete applications of certain principles. The general public knows little about these statements. In his 1942 Christmas radio message Pius XII said:

> The Church cannot ignore nor overlook the fact that the worker, in his efforts to better his lot, is opposed by a machinery which is not in accordance with nature, but is at variance with God's plan and with the purpose he had in creating the goods of this earth.

The same idea recurs in his radio message of September 1, 1944:

> The Church cannot accept those systems which recognize the rights of private property according to a completely false concept

and which are therefore opposed to a true and healthy social order. Accordingly, where, for instance, capitalism is based on such false concepts and arrogates to itself an unlimited right over property without any subordination to the common good, the Church has condemned it as contrary to the natural law.

In 1950 Pius XII first denounced the fear of some in the presence of communism, then continued:

Others show themselves no less timid and uncertain in the face of that economic system which derives its name from the excessive amassing of private wealth (excessive or exaggerated capitalism), the serious effects of which the Church has never ceased to denounce. The Church has not only indicated the abuses of capital and the right to property promoted and defended by this system, but has insisted just as often that capital and private property must be instruments of sustaining and defending the freedom and dignity of the human person.

Capitalism's basic error has been to preserve a pre-Christian concept of property. The French cardinals wrote in their letter to the Christians of France, September 8, 1949:

It should be known that in the very concept of capitalism an absolute value is given to property that does not include any consideration for the common good and the dignity of the worker. This is a materialism that is contrary to Christian teaching.[5]

This condemnation was repeated by all the French bishops in April 1954:

The French episcopacy recalls the grave condemnations pronounced by the Sovereign Pontiffs—and its own statements—against the abuses of liberal capitalism. The unlimited power that it accords to money, the unjust distribution of goods that follows, the oppression of the person by the economic system, are all gravely contrary to the laws of God. It is a duty to fight against these abuses.[6]

Notwithstanding the various economic theories that have been expounded, the unjust distribution of goods within both the developed and the underdeveloped nations has its origin in the fact that the basic ideas of economic liberalism still control our society and international relations.

In addition to the other errors of economic liberalism set forth in Development of Peoples and mentioned in the foregoing pages (an economy with profit as its motive, competition its supreme law, and absolute rights over private property), there is another fundamental error—namely, the supposition that there is automatic self regulation in the economy, by means of which, as Adam Smith wrote, "when you work for yourself, you serve society more effectively than when you work through the public interest."[7] This theory is well known: that economic activity should enjoy unlimited freedom because the profit mechanism is self-regulating in a system of free competition and automatically brings about the greatest benefits not only to the capitalist but also to the worker and to the whole of society. The important thing is to produce more and better; the rest will follow, *Armonia spontanea.* No one today accepts this idea but the mentality still persists.

Of course economic liberalism as taught and applied in past centuries no longer exists in the West; but it is still dominant in poor countries and in international dealings between rich and poor countries. If this continues, then the cleavage between the rich and the poor in the world can only grow wider.

Some authors try to defend capitalism historically, claiming that the exploitation of the worker was necessary at a certain moment in history to attain present progress. This is to make an idol of a material, industrial, and economic progress that made man a slave. Rapid growth at such a high cost was not only unnecessary, but undeniably gave rise to Marxist and communist regimes as a result of the revolt of the working classes. (If only we could get along without the automobile—and smog—for another century, in a society more humane and free from present tensions and struggles.)

VIOLENCE DOES NOT END INJUSTICES BUT CREATES OTHER FORMS

The development proposed by Paul VI is gradual, organic, and orderly. *It is progressive growth without any interruption.* This idea may be found throughout Development of Peoples but it is better expressed in Peace on Earth (*Pacem in Terris*, 1-62):

There are some souls particularly endowed with generosity, who, on finding situations where the requirements of justice are not satisfied in full, feel enkindled with the desire to change the state of things, as if they wished to have recourse to something like a revolution.

It must be borne in mind that to proceed gradually is the law of life in all its expressions. Therefore in human institutions, too, it is not possible to renovate for the better except by working from within them, gradually. *Salvation and justice are not to be found in revolution, but in evolution through concord* (Pius XII our predecessor of happy memory declared). *Violence has always achieved only destruction, not construction; the kindling of passions, not their pacification; the accumulation of hate and ruin, not the reconciliation of the contending parties. It has reduced men and parties to the difficult task of rebuilding, after sad experience, on the ruins of discord.*

Development of Peoples affirms that revolutionary insurrection is "the source of new injustices, throws more elements out of balance and brings on new disasters. A present evil should not be fought against at the cost of greater misery" (n. 31).

In this paragraph of the encyclical, the Pope acknowledged the legitimacy of a revolutionary uprising "in the case of a manifest, long-standing tyranny which would do great damage to fundamental personal rights and dangerous harm to the common good of the country." In some quarters these words were understood to be a blanket endorsement of all armed revolt, so in Bogotá, during his visit to Colombia in 1968, Paul VI took care to make his meaning perfectly clear in an address to the Latin Americans:

Many, especially among the youth, insist on the necessity of changing without delay all the social structures that they feel prevent the establishment of an effective social justice both for individuals and communities. Some are convinced that the basic problem of Latin America can be resolved only by violence.

With the same frankness that enables us to acknowledge that these theories and forms of action are often motivated ultimately in noble sentiments of justice and solidarity, we must also say, and repeat, that violence is not in the spirit of the Gospel; it is not Christian. Sudden or violent change in structures would be deceptive, inefficacious. They would certainly not be in harmony with the dignity of the people which requires that necessary changes be realized from within, that is to say, by a just awareness, by a willed decision, and by the effective *participation* of all those who are deprived because of ignorance or, at times, subhuman conditions.

Consequently, we feel that the solution of the basic problem in Latin America is to be found in a twofold, simultaneous effort that would be harmoniously and reciprocally beneficial. On the one hand assuredly to proceed to a reform of social structures, but a reform that would be gradual and suited to all. And on the other hand—and this would necessarily follow—to begin a great patient work of raising the level of human life for the majority of those who live in Latin America. To help each one to become fully conscious of his dignity, to develop his personality in the community of which he is a member and to be the conscious subject of its rights and duties, and to be freely an authentic element of economic, civic, and moral progress in the society of which he is a member. This is the great task that has priority and without which all sudden change of social structures would be artificial, useless, ephemeral, and dangerous.

Concretely, as you well know, this task consists in doing all that is possible to promote the complete development of man and his active insertion in the community: literacy, basic education, ongoing education, professional training, formation of civic and political conscience, methodical organization of material services that are essential to the normal development of individual and collective life at the present time.

In a discourse of June 7, 1967, Paul VI stated:

The Church cannot approve of those who claim to reach such a noble and legitimate goal, i.e. justice and peace on earth, through the subversion of right and social order. The Church is certainly conscious of the fact that it is bringing about a revolution with its doctrine, if by this is understood a change in mentality, a profound modification in the scale of values. The Church is perfectly aware of the strong attraction that the idea of revolution—understood as a harsh and violent change—exerts at all times on certain minds (who are eager for the absolute) as a fast, energetic and effective solution to all social problems. These minds see in it the only way that leads to justice. As a matter of fact revolutionary action usually gives birth to a whole series of injustices and sufferings because violence once unchained can be checked with difficulty and influences both people and structures. For the Church such a solution is not, therefore, the solution able to cure the evils of society.

Thus the different definitions of development given by Christian writers clearly indicate gradual evolution and not violent breaks with the past. Father Lebret says this in these words:

> For a given people and the parts of the population that make up the whole, the series of stages, from a less human phase to a more human phase according to the highest possible rate and the lowest possible cost, depends on the solidarity between the different parts of the national population and the solidarity between nations.[8]

Laurentin gives this definition:

> Progress is the process that seeks to transform each man so that he can be responsible for his own development within a community capable of bringing about its own development.[9]

U Thant, the secretary of the United Nations, gave this excellent definition of development:

> Development means growth rather than change. Change, in its turn, means social, cultural, economic, qualitative—and at the same time—quantitative modifications.[10]

In other words for the Christian, as for anyone who accepts a spiritual doctrine (that is, anyone who gives primacy of place to man and his faculties), development is a human, ongoing fact, not a violent rupture; a gradual, human growth toward freedom from hunger and oppression, not a simple change in social structure or political regimes that can be brought about by violence. If the people themselves are not prepared, then any change brought about by a violent revolt will be led by a minority and not by the unanimous thrust of people already aware of their rights. The new regime that has seized power will become a new dictatorship that will soon show that it is not much better than its predecessor and much harder to eliminate. The history of the last fifty years of violent revolt suffices to prove this.

There is much discussion today of violence and nonviolence as a means of revolution. Granted, *the Christian is for the revolution*, understood as the radical change of the present socioeconomic structure that reigns in the world; but it must be quickly added that the Christian does not wish to resort to violent methods, to effect this radical change, but seeks instead a gradual, progressive change obtained by peaceful means. Of course one cannot exclude totally and *a priori* all forms of violence. There may be certain situations and conditions where a violent insurrection could truly be the only solution; but such cases are rare, and we cannot generalize. For example, we do not believe that the present situations in Uruguay, Colombia, Venezuela and Brazil necessarily require as "the only possible solution" violent insurrection, civil war, and similar methods, although we leave to the Latin Americans the full responsibility for judging these matters for themselves.

What a Christian cannot accept is *the method of violence and violent revolt* as represented by Mao Tse-tung and Che Guevara. We do not accept the myth, the continued insistence, that war and violence are the rightful means of redeeming the third world, because we are convinced that the true revolution is not the violent one. Don Giulio Girardi has written cogently of the different positions of Christians and Marxists in regard to violence and nonviolence. He says:

The most valid argument for us is that which proposes nonviolence as the sole means of successful revolution. By this is meant a continuing revolution, simultaneously affecting social structures and human awareness, which brings about a lasting change; which has as a basis for its stability the consent of the masses; and which cannot be surrogated by violence, for the end result would be dictatorship.

Violence, even if it attains its immediate goal of changing pre-existing structures, ultimately fails to result in a successful revolution. It destroys not only material things, but morals as well, and in the release of uncontrollable forces leads to unforeseeable destruction. As a consequence the revolutionaries will be so absorbed in the work of reconstruction that they will be unable to devote themselves to the organization of new structures.

Above all, however, violence fails in the fact that it cannot foster the growth of humanism. It becomes instead an obstacle to the advance toward love and freedom because of the hate, rivalry, and disorders that invariably accompany it. Thus the stability of the newly established regime of dictatorship cannot be assured, at least not for very long. Violent action adopts the very methods it wished to abolish. It adheres in practice to the principle that might makes right. It accepts the rules of the game instead of changing them.[11]

For communism and other extremist theories, the best solution to underdevelopment is unquestionably violent revolution, class struggles, and rupture with the past. They hold that because the world is sharply divided between masters and slaves, exploiters and exploited, oppressors and oppressed, there is no possibility of reconciling the opposing classes and it is therefore logical that any attempt at reform would be a serious error. The true solutions can only come about by the overthrow of existing structures and the establishment of a dictatorship of the proletariat.

In reality history shows that violent revolution leads not to "the dictatorship *of* the proletariat" but to "dictatorship *over* the proletariat" on the part of a new class of entrenched bureaucrats. Then the only way change is possible is through purges, which are decided on the highest levels and about which the people know nothing.[12] We recall the Chinese revolution in which the twenty most prominent leaders had an average age of seventy-two years. In North Vietnam the direction of the country, even after the death of Ho Chi Minh— for twenty-five years called "the father" of his country (though popular verification of this sobriquet has never been possible)—is controlled by a triumvirate whose average age is sixty-seven years.

AUTHENTIC DEVELOPMENT RESPECTS LOCAL CULTURES

There is another important difference between the way Christians and Marxists consider development. The former hold that there should be an evolution of the local culture of a people or country. The latter think that traditional culture admits of no progress and can, though with difficulty, be eliminated.

The spiritual concept of development sees it as a human fact, and therefore one that is primarily cultural before it is technical, economical, or structural; so since it is man who is to grow and develop, man is the first agent of his own development. The importance of culture in this growth is clear. In fact, development has been defined as "culture on the march," because while it is always

changing and undergoing the most profound mutations, it nevertheless retains the special characteristics of its cultural past.

If development, therefore, is to be authentic and not alienating,
it must respect the cultural values proper to every people so that
they may be able to evolve and to adapt to different conditions
of life. The Council, recalling the Gospel message, has clearly stated
the obligation to respect the local culture (Decree on the Church's
Missionary Activity) (*Ad Gentes*), and also affirmed the right of every
people to develop according to its traditional culture (Church in
the Modern World, II, 2). Christianity offers itself as a complement
to non-Christian cultures. It does not reject them totally, but recog-
nizes that they contain many valid elements, and works so that
these elements might be preserved even within the necessary evolution.

It is true that in the past, Christians, even missionaries themselves,
have not always respected the local cultures of the people being
evangelized of colonized. In not doing so, they acted against Christian
principles and the repeated directives of the Holy See. The celebrated
"Instructions for the Propagation of the Faith," dealing with local
cultures, was written in 1659, and it is as clear and complete today
as if it had been recently written.

In our times, the popes have taken a decided position on this
matter, not only as it relates to mission evangelization but also as
it applies to the help given by rich nations to poor nations. John
XXIII has written:

> All political communities in the process of economic development
> usually have a well-defined personality on account of the re-
> sources and specific characteristics of the natural "milieu," on
> account of their traditions, which often are rich in human values,
> and lastly, on account of the typical qualities of their members.
> Political communities which are already developed, when they
> offer their help, must recognize and respect such a personality
> and overcome their temptation to force, through their help, their
> way of life on these people.

Paul VI in Development of Peoples said that in receiving help
towards development,

> . . . the receiving countries could demand that there be no inter-
> ference in their political life or subversion of their social struc-

tures. As sovereign states they have the right to conduct their own affairs, to decide on their policies and to move freely towards the kind of society they choose (n. 54).

To repeat, Marxism, contrary to the spiritual concept, holds that development is impossible without a break with the cultural past of a given country. It believes that the culture of a capitalist or feudal society is a bourgeois one that should be swept away in order to make room for the construction of a wholly new society. Therefore religion—any religion—is an alienating influence that must be done away with. In this view, then, development is not, as U Thant defined it, "growth plus change," but rather rupture with the culture of the past and the establishment of a new civilization in which all cultural institutions are made to serve the party and the interests of the proletariat. Art, motion pictures, and literature in communist lands are totally controlled by those in power. Deviationists end badly.

Marxism is particularly opposed to the traditional cultures and religions in the new countries of the third world. Where the party is not in power, the Communists do not oppose the traditional religious faiths (Islam in Indonesia, Buddhism in Burma and Ceylon, Hinduism in India, etc.), and their cultural patrimony. When they are in power, however, they set about on the methodical destruction of all vestiges of the past, with the exception of those things that have value as tourist attractions.

This calls to mind what happened in China, Tibet, and North Vietnam, where communist opposition to Buddhism, Confucianism, and the local cultures is clear and violent. The press in these countries especially condemn "the survival of the past." During the cultural revolution in China, whole libraries of ancient writings were destroyed. The same thing happened in Tibet, where—in the words of the UN's International Commission on Justice, sitting in Geneva in 1959—there had been "true physical and cultural genocide" of the Tibetan people.[13]

An eyewitness of the first few years of the Chinese communist regime writes:

> Communism wished to make a complete break with China's past, with its philosphers and literary men. It fought not only Confucianists but Taoists as well, and declared merciless war against

those intellectuals who were considered the guardians of the past. At first they tried to reduce all to Marxist obedience by means of brainwashing and other drastic measures of ideological oppression. . . . Then when they saw that these intellectuals would not yield, they prevented them from teaching and sought to eliminate them entirely by numerous purges.[14]

An expert and student of black Africa, Dr. Louis-Paul Aujoulat, wrote that the attraction of Marxism, while continuing to be strong in Africa, has recently diminished, not because of the meager achievements that communist countries were able to offer Africa,

but simply because the Marxists give to the people of Asia and Africa the impression that they are bringing them a world that is all finished with the possibility that a country could fully realize its own development by means of a social and cultural promotion suddenly imposed upon them. While the West offers as separate elements the achievements of technology, industrial structures, or other things, Marxism pretends to construct a whole edifice that it offers to appease the hope and longing of disinherited people.[15]

AMBIGUITY AND THE MYTH OF PROGRESS

There is a last basic difference between the Christian and the materialist concepts of development. The latter have a blind faith in man and inspire an ingenuous belief in mankind's continuous progress and a permanent betterment of the world as indisputable fact. They generally believe that the world is inevitably advancing toward better days, toward total development that will bring peace, abundance, and justice.

The Christian is not equally optimistic. The Church, like its divine Master, has not placed complete confidence in man since it knows that just as, with God's help, man is capable of every heroism, he is, because of the damage caused by original sin, capable of every brutality. If development were merely a technical, scientific, economic fact, it might be possible to share the general optimism. But *development is above all a human and a moral fact* that should be expressed on the political-social plane rather than on a technical-scientific one. In this area it is not true that mankind is advancing automatically toward better days and toward less inhuman ways of living together.

In other words, while technical-scientific progress is without a doubt continuous and irreversible, it is a proved and certain fact that moral and political-social progress is not. Therefore we ought to be aware that development is an ambiguous fact. This is clearly stated in Development of Peoples:

> Increased possession is not the ultimate goal of nations or of individuals. All growth is ambivalent. It is essential if man is to develop as a man, but in a way it imprisons man if he considers it the supreme good, and it restricts his vision. Then we see hearts harden and minds close, and men no longer gather together in friendship but out of self-interest, which soon leads to oppositions and disunity. The exclusive pursuit of possessions thus becomes an obstacle to individual fulfillment and to man's true greatness. Both for nations and for individual men, avarice is the most evident form of moral underdevelopment (n. 19).

The consequences are obvious:

> If further development calls for the work of more and more technicians, even more necessary is the deep thought and reflection of wise men in search of a new humanism which will enable modern man to find himself anew by embracing the higher values of love and friendship, of prayer and contemplation. This is what will permit the fullness of authentic development, a development which is for each and all the transition from less human conditions to those which are more human (*Ibid.*, 20).

So it is necessary to warn men against an ingenuous and facile optimism in the future of mankind according to the great myth that prevailed in the nineteenth century, and in spite of all the disillusionment that man had experienced concerning an end to war, racism, dictatorial and oppressive systems, etc., has continued until our own. There is a Christian pessimism in the Gospel. Recall the parable of the simultaneous growth of the wheat and the weeds and those words of Christ: "When the Son of Man comes, do you think he will find faith on the earth?" (Lk. 18:8). And also, "Many false prophets will arise, and will mislead many; and as lawlessness is, men's love for one another will grow cold" (Mt. 24:12-13).

The Church in the Modern World, which is full of confidence in man and of optimism about the future of mankind, the Council well expresses the Christian version of progress:

Sacred Scripture teaches the human family what the experience of the ages confirms: that while human progress is a great advantage to man, it brings with it a strong temptation. For when the order of values is jumbled, and bad is mixed with the good, individuals and groups pay heed solely to their own interests, and not to those of others. Thus it happens that the world ceases to be a place of true brotherhood. In our own day, the magnified power of humanity threatens to destroy the race itself.

For a monumental struggle against the powers of darkness pervades the whole history of man. The battle was joined from the very origins of the world and will continue until the last day, as the Lord has attested. Caught in this conflict, man is obliged to wrestle constantly if he is to cling to what is good. Nor can he achieve his own integrity without valiant efforts and the help of God's grace.

That is why Christ's Church, trusting in the design of the Creator, acknowledges that human progress can serve man's true happiness. Yet she cannot help echoing the Apostle's warning: "Be not conformed to this world" (Rom. 12:2). By the world is here meant that spirit of vanity and malice which transforms into an instrument of sin those human energies intended for the service of God and man (n. 37).

A theologian, Father Cattui de Menasce, wrote in a lucid statement on "Social Progress and Ethical Progress":

The mystery of the cross can exist not only for the individual but also for the community. Therefore, let us realize that the Christian idea of progress does not necessarily mean triumphalism. Communists think they know where history is going. We do not know, and we say this tranquilly. We do not know where the history of mankind is going, but we know where the history of the salvation of the world is going. We know that it is advancing towards happiness beyond this world, in the hereafter. This is our idea, not an earthly messianism according to the pattern of a Teilhard or of a certain progressive Catholicism which confuses the idea of progress of the world with the idea of progress that finds its good in another world. Let us realize that they are not the same things. For us the progress of the world can be this—I hope that it will be this—but maybe it will not.[16]

If there is a Christian pessimism that contrasts with the optimism of those who believe that technical-scientific progress is enough to bring man to all happiness, there is also a Christian optimism diametrically opposed to the nihilism that, in the presence of some of the horrors of our age, has inspired a whole literature on the decadence of civilization as well as movements engaged in "global disputes" that deprive man of all hope and every reason for living.

The Christian is especially charged with being moderate but today not a few Christians, notably among the youth, act as if such an adjuration is extremely displeasing to them. Certainly an agreement must be reached about the meaning of the word. The Christian is moderate because, on the one hand, he is aware of man's limits and of the impossibility of attaining total peace and absolute justice on this earth; but on the other hand, he also has complete confidence in the grace of God that redeems and sustains man and offers him every opportunity to construct a better world. Thus the Christian rejected the deification of man and the myth that man is sufficient unto himself and can be content with purely material and human progress; and by so doing, he is spared the radical pessimism of the man who, trusting solely in man, has no further confidence in a better future.

The myth of progress, which in origin is as much liberal capitalist as Marxist, is based on the presupposition that man redeems himself, and therefore in the end the redemption brought by the Son of God is not necessary. We have on the one hand the excessive trust in the purely human messianism of a perfect society; on the other hand, the contact with the delusion of history, together with the recurring wickedness of man, brings the temptation of nihilism and total mistrust in man and in the future of mankind. If one rejects original sin and then the divine redemption of man, the history of man becomes an incomprehensible mystery.

In a word, *the crisis in contemporary civilization derives from progress without God* as John XXIII wrote in *Christianity and Social Progress* with words unexpectedly severe in so meek and good a man:

However, no folly seems more characteristic of our time than the desire to establish a firm and meaningful temporal order, but without God, its necessary foundation. Likewise, some wish to proclaim the greatness of man, but with the source dried up from which such greatness flows and receives nourishment: that is, by impeding and, if it were possible, stopping the yearning of souls for God. But the turn of events in our times, whereby the hopes of many are shattered and not a few have come to grief, unquestionably confirm the words of Scripture: "Unless the Lord build the house, they labor in vain who build it"(Ps. 126, 1) (n. 217).

Let us conclude with these words from The Church in the Modern World:

Hence if anyone wants to know how this unhappy situation can be overcome, Christians will tell him that all human activity, constantly imperiled by man's pride and deranged self-love, must be purified and perfected by the power of Christ's cross and resurrection (n. 37).

FOOTNOTES

1. R. Dickinson, *La règle et le niveau.* C.E.C., Geneva, 1968, p. 11.

2. "Vision chrétienne des déséquilibres économiques et sociaux," a conference held in May 1963 at the SIIAEC congress (Secrétariat Intern. des Ingégnieurs des Agronomes et des Cadres Economiques Catholiques), in *Responsables,* September/October 1963, p. 20.

3. *Marxismo e cristianesimo,* Cittadella, Assisi, 1966, p. 232.

4. Jean-Paul Sartre and Roger Garaudy, the French communist intellectuals, have courageously affirmed that communism has reduced man, on the basis of the principles of materialism, to the level of a mere object, a slave of the state system. *See* V. Fagone, "Ideologia e prassi del communismo: le regioni del dissenso di Sartre e di Garaudy" in *La Civiltà Cattolica,* March 7, 1970, pp. 448-462. Garaudy, the theorist of French communism, who was expelled from the party as a result of his disapproval of what took place in Czechoslovakia, has spoken out strongly against the crushing of the human person by the communist system and his own French Communist party. *See* R. Garaudy, *Tutta la Verità,* Mondadori, Milan, 1970.

5. Cited in Van Gestel, *La dottrina sociale della Chiesa,* Città Nuova, Rome, 1965, p. 561.

6. *Documentation Catholique,* Paris, 1955, col. 744.

7. E. James, *Storia del pensiero economico,* Garzanti, Milan, 1963, p. 91.

8. *Progresso e solidarietà fra i popoli,* Borla, Turin, 1967, pp. 86-87.

9. *Liberation, Development and Salvation,* Orbis, Maryknoll, N.Y. 1972, p. 51.

10. *The United Nations Development Decade,* United Nations, New York, 1961, p. 2.

11. *Cristiani e marxisti a confronto sulla pace*, Cittadella, Assisi, 1967, p. 61. *See also* the eighth brochure (most especially the first chapter, pp. 11-20) of Don Mazzolari, *Rivoluzione cristiana*, La Locusta, Vicenza, 1967.

12. This is particularly true of communist regimes. All without exception were born in violent revolution. *See* M. Gilas, *La nuova classe, Un' analisi del sistema communista*, Il Mulino. Bologna, 1957. Moreover, even aside from regimes, history has not yet provided an example of a violent revolution that did not lead to a dictatorship with the exception of some anticolonial wars, fought by a whole people against the dominating foreigners—for example, America's war of independence, the war in the Philippines, etc.

13. *See* especially the volume: *Le Tibet et la République Populaire de Chino, Rapport présenté à la Commission International de Jusistes par le Comité Juridique d'enquête sur la question de Tibet*, International Commission of Jurists, Geneva, 1960, p. 366.

14. A. Crotti, *Il popolo cinese di fronte al comunisme*, PIME, Milan, 1962, p. 25. *Also see* A. Lazzarotto, *La cultura cinese "concime" della revoluzione maoista*, Stadium, Rome, June, 1970, pp. 5-18. The same tactics used in China to eliminate culture and traditional religion were also applied to North Vietnam under the regime of Ho Chi Minh.

15. *Action sociale et développement*, Colin, Paris, 1969, p. 283.

16. *Progresso sociale e progresso etico*, No. 10, Coscienza, Rome, 1969, pp. 242-247.

THE FOUR
REVOLUTIONS THAT
DEVELOPED THE
WESTERN WORLD

2

In the first chapter of our study we asked: What is development? We stressed the difference between the Christian (or spiritual) concept and the materialistic. Now we must ask: What is underdevelopment and why does it occur? In the final chapter we shall see what true commitment for development is and how it corresponds to man's true vocation and needs.

THE MARCH FORWARD AND THE SIGN OF DEVELOPMENT

Development and underdevelopment are fairly new and relative terms—new, because only a few centuries ago, all countries were more or less static, and hence neither developed nor underdeveloped; the distinction was born when some began to develop themselves. The terms are relative inasmuch as development and underdevelopment must be considered in relation to different situations in various countries or continents. To give a concrete example, Italy, in comparison to the Congo or to Burma, is a developed country. Yet compared to Sweden and the United States, it is underdeveloped. But Sweden and the United States are also "on the march to development," because they have not yet attained the optimum conditions that enable man to develop himsef integrally. And this point will never be reached. The potentialities of man—who is created in the

27

image and likeness of God—are almost infinite and we do not yet
know what they encompass.

A. Barrère, President of the French Social Weeks, has written:

> Development is a process of establishing values in a society where,
> because of the improvement in material conditions a fulfillment
> of being is possible for the individual and the collectivity. . . .
> This is the progressive march towards a better humanity. . . .
> This is a continuing evolution. It has an end but it does not
> come to an end.[1]

Development, therefore, is not a goal, a state to which one can
arrive in a definitive way, but a continuous "march forward" of
man and society towards perfect fulfillment. In this sense, as was
pointed out in Chapter One, no land, and no people, are ever fully
developed, but are forever advancing towards new frontiers which
are discovered along the way.

Relatively speaking, we can say a society is developed when the
"forward advance" enables it to offer its members whatever is necessary for their complete fulfillment: the basic conditions for a human
life (food, home, school, work, security, etc.) and freedom from
any kind of oppression or barriers, including psychological ones.
No society is yet able to offer every man all that is necessary for
his integral development, and as we have said, none will ever be
developed in the absolute sense because the potentiality for man's
development, especially from an intellectual and spiritual point of
view, is practically unlimited.

The sign of a society's development, then, is the march forward,
the movement toward concrete opportunities for betterment. And
if we look at the different countries of the world we see that some
are advancing, some are standing still, and others, perhaps, are going
backwards.

Normally the distinctive signs of underdeveloped lands (if we
assume that these signs are partly true but not exhaustive) reside
in the annual per capita income, the availability of proteins and
calories per person, and the illiteracy rate, for example. These, when
deficient, are aspects of underdevelopment, but they do not include
the totality of the phenomenon. To us it seems more exact to apply
the term "underdeveloped" to those lands that are not able to offer
their inhabitants the basic conditions for human growth and are

not yet on the way toward realizing them. Or they are advancing so slowly that they are, in effect, standing still, since population growth sometimes outruns material progress.

The basis of all integral development is the growth of man and the conditions that make this growth possible: sufficient food, sanitary measures, education, homes, stable employment, fair wages, political and religious freedom, etc. These conditions are precisely those that are lacking in so many lands and continents that we incorrectly say are on the way to development. As the Most Reverend Manuel Larrain, late, lamented bishop of Talca, Chile, said, referring to Latin America: "To speak realistically we should say that these lands are on the way to a growing underdevelopment."

MARXIST AND CAPITALIST THEORIES
DO NOT EXPLAIN UNDERDEVELOPMENT

We have said that development signifies people marching forward toward their integral fulfillment, while underdevelopment means people at a standstill. The question arises: Why, at a certain moment of history, have some people and lands begun to advance, while others have not moved?

In the distant past the whole of human society was more or less standing still on the road to development. Among the various peoples underdevelopment took different forms: scarcity of food, inhumane social structures, illiteracy, slavery. In some societies women were not considered to be persons, and the lower classes were without any rights whatsoever. In other words, no country, no society, in the past offered all its citizens human conditions for life, and none was about to do so. They did not see any need to give opportunities for education, economic progress, and freedom to the slave, the worker in the field, the lower classes, or women.

This static condition (or underdevelopment) was not incompatible with great progress in the arts, literature, or philosophy. An elite group enjoyed favorable conditions for a human life and had cultivated artistic expression and thinking; but society as a whole was denied access to opportunities, which were rightfully theirs, to progress. Again we ask, *why at a certain moment did some people begin to advance, while others did not?* Where did this forward thrust towards progress come from? This is the fundamental question for anyone who wishes to understand the mechanism of the development and the underdevelopment of peoples and for anyone who wishes to take part in the struggle against hunger and want.

Let us say at once that we are dealing with a highly complex problem because it involves a number of historical facts and their interpretation. It would therefore be an oversimplification to give a categorical response that would explain everything by an *a priori* theory meant to apply to every case in the world. Marxism, for example, commits this error when it tries to explain the backwardness of certain people by the theory of classes, and claims that under-developed people exist because developed people have oppressed and exploited them. A theory such as this offers many advantages. It is simple, clear to all, provides a scapegoat for every unpleasant situation, and suggests that the class struggle as proposed by Marxism is the means of man's liberation. It is in fact a theory widely accepted even by Christians, especially by young people and those who know little about the world. It has, however, a serious defect. It does not correspond to historic reality, and as we shall see, it does not stand the test of reality.

On the other hand, the capitalist thesis on underdevelopment has led to the long-held belief that underdevelopment has been, and is, principally due to the scarcity of natural resources or capital; therefore outside help can solve everything. But this explanation is both oversimplified and untrue. As Sauvy has written:

> After many trials and errors, economists of every land, even of America, have come to the conclusion that the origin of development is not money, as was so long believed, not capital, but culture—men's ability to know how to enjoy their natural riches. Chinese wisdom expressed this very evident fact ages ago: Give a man a fish and let him eat it for one day and you have taught him to fish and to eat for his whole life.[2]

THE REVOLUTION OF IDEAS

If it is true that man is "the initiator of development," as we have just said, then it is also true that underdevelopment is not the result of a deficiency in man (this would be a form of racism, because it presumes that some people are constitutionally superior to others), but due instead to a delay along the various avenues of human culture, in its expression as conditioned by circumstances, history, religion, etc.

In general, studies of underdevelopment gloss over the historic aspect. They limit themselves to the present situation and the increasing differences between people on the way to development and underdeveloped people, looking for causes in present-day facts, such as international trade, neocolonial relations, etc. But these facts cannot explain the deep motives, the historic causes, that have enabled some people to begin their advance towards development while others remain stationary.

The central fact that should be clarified (and that represents the key to the whole discussion about development) is the initial point of departure: *Why have some people started to move forward while others remain motionless, static?*

Here are the essential differences between the histories of rich and poor people.[3] The former have experienced four revolutions that the latter have never known. These revolutions have started them on the road of development:

1. *The first revolution on the plane of ideas* (ideas make history) is the one brought out by the concepts of the equality of all men and the dignity of each individual person. This revolutionary idea affected the society of masters and slaves, in which the slave was considered to be on the level of a domestic animal without rights or personality. Western society was radically changed by the Judaeo-Christian religion which gave a correct idea of man and his relation to God and nature: man created in the image of God; man, king of creation, and with an end superior to that of any other creature; man free to determine and shape his own destiny—these are all basic ideas, derived from biblical revelation, on which our civilization rests. Christianity, offering the example of God-made-man, has suggested the possibility of man's limitless ascent enabling him to share in the life of God by means of grace. This is the initial step—recognition of the dignity of each single human person—toward man's progress and that of society.

In other words, in the West, man at the center of creation, thinking and acting, became the essential nucleus around which everything else is organized. When this idea, slowly maturing over the centuries, was accepted, it put an end to the immobility of society and of mentality, and started the movement toward liberty, democracy, socialism, and social justice.

The idea that man is the center of creation seems obvious to us, but to others this is not so. We shall see that in the society and traditional cultures of the third world, man is only one of the many elements of nature without any particular superior dignity. It is clear that, starting from such a basic idea, man could not progress but remained stationary and closed in the recurring cycles of nature.

2. *The second revolution is that of the idea of progress*, the advance towards a level of life more worthy of man and the full recognition of his human person. This second revolution in traditional thought follows from the first; if man is the king of creation, if man is made in the image of God, this man of so lofty a dignity ought to progress, ought to construct a better future by dominating nature, making it serve his needs. The West would never have begun the forward advance that we know today had it not discovered, at a certain point in its history, the sovereign dignity of man over all creation, the fundamental equality of all men, and the messianic vision of a better world to be constructed with his own hands and the help of others. This idea of progress has given Western culture an ideal, has broken down psychological barriers, and created a dynamic tension towards the future.

Christianity, becoming the spirit of Western culture, transmitted to it hope in the future, an eschatological and totally religious hope but one which was also seen in human and earthly terms as man's path towards his lofty destiny. For the Christian or for the Christianized man, even though he be an atheist, history is a path forward, and the commitment of life is to progress and to make mankind progress because the potentialities of man created in the image of God are infinite and therefore always capable of still further development.[4]

For non-Christian or pre-Christian culture, on the contrary, history is a continued return to the past, a closed circle that repeats itself like the seasons, like the mythical serpent devouring its own tail. Our progressive mentality is a new fact in the history of man that has not yet gained popular acceptance in the third world, just as it was almost unknown in the ancient Western world. Marcus

Aurelius, one of the wisest men of Roman antiquity, declared that a man of forty had already seen and experienced all that there was to see and to experience in the world. Life could have nothing new to offer him. In the works of this great man of the past we find no sense of the continued progress of mankind, no new frontiers to be reached, no ideal of a better future to be achieved. The dominant idea of some civilizations is not movement forward but no movement at all.

THE CULTURAL BASIS OF SCIENCE AND TECHNOLOGY

3. *The third revolution is that of population growth.* When the idea of the dignity of man (made in the image of God) and of man's dominion over nature is united to the idea of progress and work towards a better future, it results in the development of medical science. Man becomes the center of experimentation to improve the conditions of, and to prolong, his life. Gradually assuring man better health, medicine leads to a growth in population, which, in its turn, upsets the economic balance of mere subsistence in which men had hitherto lived.

In the West, population growth is an extremely positive element of socioeconomic development (the opposite, as we shall see, of what has taken place in the third world); in fact the population increases in a situation that is prepared to receive all its efforts towards a better organization of its productive forces, thus setting in motion a whole series of powerful causes and effects in the field of economics that have brought about the material progress of our society.

The same thing has happened with social progress. Growing numbers of workers, farmers, and members of the lower classes, conscious of their dignity, stand before the footlights of society asking for greater social justice in a way that would not have been possible solely through the benevolent condescension of the upper classes. Population growth, coupled with the awareness of man's dignity and the fundamental equality of all men, has given the impetus not only to material progress and productivity but also to social progress, to democracy, and to socialism. However, we shall see that in the third world population growth has had other results. There it has not led to greater productivity or greater social justice, because there men were unaware of their dignity and equality.

4. *The fourth and last revolution concerns science and technology*, which have made possible the economic development to which we alluded above. In this case, as in that of the development of medical science and all the sciences focusing on man, the first step follows from the first two revolutions, that of ideas: the dignity of man, "king of creation," and the idea of holding dominion over nature so that it will serve and benefit man. All these ideas which seem to us so obvious are in fact a novelty in human history and have not yet reached the majority of men in the third world.

In the West the discovery of nature and its progressive control by means of science and technology are phenomena of recent centuries. They could not have occurred without any planning, but were the product of a whole culture that was headed in that direction. This also explains why it is so difficult for science and technology to be accepted and adapted when transplanted to the people of another culture. It is a fact that, at first sight, a Westerner cannot succeed in understanding a mentality profoundly different from his own, precisely because he does not understand its culture.

This explains the mistakes made by many experts in technical assistance to poor lands. They believed that all they had to do was to bring to these people the tools of modern production and that at once the people would begin to produce, working like men in Western countries. This is a materialist vision of development which gives greater importance to man's tools than to man himself. The economist J. H. Frankel writes:

> Technical knowledge never exists in the abstract but only in the passing form appropriate to a momentary situation and to the unique problems to which these are adapted. . . . This determines the reactions of man to the many changing problems occasioned by the environment and the presence of other men. This is why technical knowledge cannot easily be transferred from one situation to another, unless the individual is able to adapt it to a new kind of activity.[5]

Western technology and science are bound to a whole culture; they are the product of slowly maturing thought and have transformed the mentality, the habits, and society itself. In the third world, on the other hand, products are shipped or imported from outside and have no local cultural basis, consequently they produce serious psychological traumas and are accepted only in part and with much difficulty. One of the fundamental differences between the Western world and the third world is precisely this: On one side are societies that have had a long cultural preparation, culminating in modern progress; on the other side are those who are unprepared for the break with the whole cultural past that would result from the introduction of new revolutionary ideas and new technology.

Technical and scientific discoveries have enabled the West to advance economically in agricultural and industrial production, but there was a bourgeois class ready to make use of these discoveries. Yves Lacoste, a student of non-Western civilization, writes:

> The principal cause of the economic development of Great Britain is to be found in the existence of a group of men gifted with a productive mentality that was able to master these inventions and to create conditions such as would guarantee that the new object would produce relative results with the greatest possible profit. These entrepreneurs came mostly from the bourgeoisie.[6]

The birth of the bourgeoisie in the West was not a fortuitous fact but the result of the development of the whole society that little by little broke the rigid pattern of the past: the sharp division between rich and poor, nobles and plebeians, freemen and slaves. There followed a mixing of classes and the birth of new classes, among which the bourgeoisie is a sign of the dynamism of Western society that does not cling to patterns of the past.

In the third world society did not evolve. It has not seen the birth of new classes with a more progressive spirit. Until the contact began with the West, everything remained just as it was—the rigid tribal patterns, the castes, the rulers. Lacoste also wrote:

> An historical fact of great importance characterizes all the lands that are now underdeveloped: the absence of a bourgeoisie. Whatever be the level of civilization that may have been reached . . . the factors of the formation and development of a bourgeoisie have not appeared. . . . The absence of a dynamic social class, eager to overthrow to its own advantage the established order, has made the realization of an economic revolution impossible.[7]

CHRISTIANITY IS THE SOURCE OF MODERN PROGRESS

What we want to stress in this chapter is *the West developed in virtue of an inner thrust and not because of outside influences.* As Barbara Ward has written, the four revolutions that are at the basis of modern progress "were all born in the North Atlantic area, in nations located on the borders of the North Atlantic. England, the United States, and Western Europe, working and developing together, created a new type of human society."[8]

We cannot know for certain the reasons why the West completed these four revolutions, especially the two most important ones, concerning ideas. Lady Ward attributes the initial inspiration for the revolutionary idea of progress to Christianity, since in the West these ideas (the dignity of the single individual, equality among all men, the progress of history) were unknown in pre-Christian civilization. This claim does not seem completely proved historically but it is repeated by many other authors, some of whom state that the Christian idea could easily flourish in soil prepared by the Graeco-Roman civilization. Two students of civilization explain it this way:

> To all that has sprung from the Graeco-Roman world and above all to Christianity, Western civilization is indebted from the point of view of equality, freedom, and fraternal charity for an approach to life unknown in other civilizations. The ancient and modern reaction against slavery, the struggle against despotism, the establishment of political and social democracy, the rights of man, and the other forms of respect for the human person remain the original acquisition of the West, in spite of applications often excessive or suspect.[9]

Christianity in the West has profoundly influenced the culture and its basic foundations. It cannot be said that the West acts according to the principles of the Gospel, but our civilization is permeated by Christianity (communism is even said to be *a Christian heresy*; in the third world it can be clearly seen that communism is derived from Christianity and that it could not have come from Buddhist or Hindu cultures).

The philosopher Karl Jaspers has written:

> Every time the question is asked whether Europe could exist and could possibly be without the Bible, but solely on its pre-

biblical and Greek origins, the answer must always be that whatever we are, we are as the result of this biblical religion and
the secularization that results from this religion, from the bases
of finest humanism to the motivations of modern science and
the principal leaders of the great philosophies. In fact, without
the Bible we fall into nothing.[10]

The Christian influence on the West is said to be so decisive
that without it, Western history could not be explained and the
Western world could not exist as a cultural bloc with common basic
elements. In other words, Christianity has given to Western culture—and it has given it as revealed religion—a historic sense of
the world and a sense of human dignity that other cultures do not
have. It has created the basis of progress.

Christopher Dawson, in his work *Religion and Culture*,[11] sees in
Christianity the first cause of the modern progress of science, because
it is Christianity that freed man from enslavement to nature, gave
him knowledge of his dignity, and a messianic hope to fight for—that
is, a goal to approach in history and beyond. This is also the thought
of Arnold Toynbee, Max Weber, and others. Cardinal John Henry
Newman thought[12] that the importance of Christianity for the Western world was to be found above all in the fact that the doctrine
of Christ brought man knowledge of his nature, his dignity, and
the meaning of his development. This explains the progress of the
West through the centuries.[13]

WESTERN FORMS OF MODERN PROGRESS
ARE NOT ALWAYS POSITIVE

Modern progress born in the West and carried to the rest of the
world is not integrally positive and therefore cannot be identified
with the integral development of man of which we spoke in the
preceding chapter. The West, moreover, has betrayed its spiritual
Christian matrix, and has ended in creating a form of progress largely
materialistic, whether in its liberal-capitalism or Marxist-communist
version.

Therefore we must face this paradoxical situation: On one side
Western civilization and modern progress are derived from the Christian principles of the dignity of man and the equality of all men,

thus effecting undeniable progress in our concepts and models of life not based on revelation; on the other side this same Western civilization and this same modern progress have in practice denied the Christian inspiration which gave it its initial impulse, thus offering a rather negative picture for an authentic integral human development. There is danger that the people of the third world, blindly following the models of development of the West, will end by betraying, as did the West, the spiritual values inherited from the past.

John XXIII and Paul VI have clearly warned against this danger in their social encyclicals. We read in Christianity and Social Progress:

> Scientific and technological progress, economic development, betterment in living conditions are certainly positive elements in a civilization. But we must remember that they are not and that they cannot be considered supreme values, because they are only means to an end. We notice with sorrow in economically developed countries that there are many human beings who have either subdued, extinguished or turned upside down their hierarchy of values. These human beings neglect, forget or deny spiritual values while they praise progress in science, technology, economic development and material well-being. For them these material values have become all important and even their only aim in life. This fact constitutes a disintegrating danger within the help that the economically developed people give to the people in process of economic development, who traditionally keep very much alive the most important human values. It is therefore essentially immoral to try to destroy these values; they should instead be respected, as far as possible clarified, and developed so that they can remain what they essentially are: the basis of a true civilization.

In Development of Peoples, Paul VI, after admonishing poor people not to lose their deep cultural values in their search for progress and material benefits alone, writes:

> Disadvantaged peoples can never be sufficiently on their guard against this temptation which comes to them from wealthy nations. For these nations all too often set an example of success in a highly technical and culturally developed civilization; they also provide the model for a way of acting that is principally aimed at the conquest of material prosperity. Not that material

prosperity of itself precludes the activity of the human spirit. On the contrary, the human spirit, "increasingly free of its bondage to creatures, can be more easily drawn to the worship and contemplation of the Creator." However, "modern civilization itself often complicates the approach to God, not for any essential reason, but because it is excessively engrossed in earthly affairs." Developing nations must know how to discriminate among those things that are held out to them; they must be able to assess critically, and eliminate those deceptive goods which would only bring about a lowering of the human ideal, and to accept those values that are sound and beneficial, in order to develop them alongside their own, in accordance with their own genius (n. 41).

FOOTNOTES

1. "Le développement à l'échelle mondiale," *Le développement, la justice et la paix*, 54 Semaine Sociale, Nantes, 1967, Chronique Sociale de France, Lyons, 1967, p. 11.

2. In *Le Monde*, Paris, March 12, 1964.

3. Barbara Ward, *The Rich Nationa and the Poor Nations*, Norton, New York, 1962.

4. Let us note, lest we be misunderstood, that when we say that Christianity and the Christian are progressive, we do not mean to say that all Christians are progressive, much less that the Christian church has always favored progress. In fact, history often shows the exact opposite. Here we are speaking of the Judaeo-Christian biblical message that has revolutionized Western culture.

5. *The Economic Impact on Underdeveloped Societies*, Cambridge, Mass., Harvard University Press, 1955, p. 24.

6. *Geographia del sottosviluppo*, Mondadori, Milan, 1968, p. 227.

7. *Op. cit.*, p. 232.

8. *Op. cit.*, p. 16.

9. Laloup and Nelis, *Culture et Civilisation*, Casterman, Tournai, 1957, p. 114.

10. Cited in Koenig, "La religion et la culture," *Documentation Catholique*, 1965, col. 909.

11. New York, Sheed and Ward, 1948, p. 47.

12. *Apologia*, 865, pp. 245, 253; *Essays critical and historical*, 1871, p. 96.

13. The message of Christ is the liberation of man and the source of progress. There is need to guard against a superficial triumphalism—not that we can always say this of the Church of Christ, which has, at certain times and places, been somewhat of an obstacle to progress. Some examples: the prohibition of interest on loans; the tendency to amass wealth; the cult of resignation and patience (which can turn into fatalism); the repression of the will, of desires, of freedom of thought, and of freedom of research; the collusion of the Church with the most backward classes, etc. What may be said of the message of Jesus cannot be applied in its entirety to the Church and to Christians.

WHY HAS
THE THIRD WORLD
NOT DEVELOPED?

3

If the man in the street is asked why Africa is underdeveloped, he will say something like this: "Because colonialism, racism, and exploitation by the whites have created such conditions of extreme poverty that it is difficult today for these people to rise." This is the answer given not only by people without special training, but also by students, newspapermen, and writers who should be better informed.

Fifty years ago during the height of the colonial period, Europeans believed that they were bringing civilization to the primitive people of Africa—that is, to barbarians, to uncivilized, scarcely complete men. They made the mistake of measuring other cultures against the standards of their own and judging anything different from their own to be inferior.[1] Today we are repeating the same mistake of thinking that poverty and the different human conditions of people in the third world depend on the West, and these people are not to be the subjects, but the objects, in their own history in which we are always the principal rulers: yesterday to bring civilization, today to bring exploitation and poverty. To sum up, we will begin to understand something about the third world when we are freed from our ethnocentrism. This is the mania of looking on ourselves as the center of the world on which all else depends.

The same mistake is made when it is thought that the chief contribution to the development of the third world should come from rich countries, whereas before all else, development is the result of the people themselves moving in the right direction, albeit with help from outside. But this help will be worth nothing if there is not an inner drive towards development.

INTERNAL AND EXTERNAL CAUSES OF UNDERDEVELOPMENT

Let us recall the question asked previously: Why is Africa, or to put it more generally, why is the third world underdeveloped? In the preceding chapter we explained why the West is developed. Now we must try to understand why the rest of the world has not made the slow ascent towards modern progress, at least not until the last decade.

There are two kinds of causes that explain this fact—*causes from within the third world and causes from without*. First we will consider the internal causes.

We know that the phenomenon of underdevelopment is very complex. In a general way we can say that the third world did not develop because it did not experience the four revolutions that carried the West to development, especially the revolution of ideas that transformed and dynamized Western people, leading them to science, technology, modern organization of society and production, and the establishment of the great principles of democracy and social justice. In the traditional cultures of these third-world countries, there was no drive towards these revolutions. The initial drive came from outside, from contacts with the West, but even today it has not yet reached the majority of people, who continue to live according to traditional forms and mentalities. The demographic revolution was the only one that had an immediate success in the third world; this took place, however, without any revolution of ideas, of organization of society, or of technical production. Therefore, the third world has found it hard to get started on the road to development.

Let us try to be more exact about the causes of the third world's inability to move toward development. This is not an easy thing to do because we are dealing with other related factors—not economic, technical, or social factors that can be grasped at once—but cultural factors. It is extremely difficult for a man of one culture to understand the conditions created by another. The man in the street thinks that Africans have our mentality, our way of reasoning and our kind of training, and it is just by chance that their skin is black. As a matter of fact, the difference in color is the least of all the differences that separate a Caucasian from an African or a Chinese. The real difference is to be found in the vast cultural and intellectual diversity. This is a difference harder to understand, but it is also the one that explains the different paths of various peoples and lands.

Now development, or its opposite—immobility—depends on the people's concept of life and the basic ideas of their culture. Let us look at some concrete cases.

FAULTY UNDERSTANDING OF THE RELATIONS BETWEEN MAN AND GOD, MAN AND NATURE

In Western culture the influence of Judaeo-Christian thought has placed the accent on *the transcendence of God*. Man is the king of creation, although he does not belong to the world beyond nature. He is made to God's image and therefore is infinitely superior to all other creatures who are at his service. Man has the historical task of controlling nature and of constructing on earth a just society worthy of man. This is the drive behind all scientific discoveries, explorations, exploitations of nature, and other human achievements.

In non-Western cultures, God is looked on as *immanent in the world*. All reality is mythologized or divinized. Man is on the lowest step of the supernatural world, the prisoner of matter. His destiny is to free himself and become spirit, to lose himself in God. This explains the Buddhist *struggle against desires*. Desire causes suffering, because it leads man to matter, not to spirit. If man suppresses desire, he separates himself from matter and suffering, and goes to God. It is a lack of faith in matter, the body, and nature, that are seen as obstacles to the attainment of the spirit. (Even in Christianity there have been heresies of this kind.) This is why in Hinduism, the asceticism of Yoga frees one from desire; the principle of Maya is that all is illusion; and adherents of metempsychosis propound the doctrine of continual rebirth that frees man from his body so that he may attain to God and lose his identity in God. In other words, non-Western cultures did not find the right concepts of man and the relations between man and God. They did not recognize man's rightful autonomy and therefore did not understand why man wanted to be concerned about material things when his only purpose was to free himself from them and turn to God.

In contrast to this false concept of the relation between man and nature, Western man looks on nature as a gift from God to be enjoyed, explored, and controlled, and thus it should serve to elevate man. This is so plain, so obvious, that any other way of thinking seems impossible.

For a man of the third world—and naturally I am not thinking of one who has received a modern education in the West—nature is to be contemplated, feared, submitted to, respected. In many cultures and religions nature is divinized; therefore to transform it or to treat it violently would be an evil. Father Bertolucci, a missionary in Burundi and a student of African culture, writes:

> The Africans, before they were brought out of their isolation, did not look for progress, but for balance, maintenance of the status quo. They were not preoccupied with progress, and they wanted no changes. They did not want to control nature, but to respect and adapt themselves to it. To want to transform or correct nature would seem to the African an act of arrogance against the mysterious forces that rule over nature itself.[2]

During my travels in Africa, or any other country, missionaries have said to me on different occasions: "I cannot bring a tractor here. The concept these people have of nature as something divine to be respected cannot be brutally violated. The change must come about little by little, preserving a certain contemplative value and a respect for the elements of nature."

Noel Drogat, a sociologist, has made on-the-spot studies of the conditions of the Afro-Asiatic peoples. He writes:

> For many peasants, Asiatics or Africans, agriculture, unlike technology, is a religious act. These beliefs are rooted in every aspect of the life of the man in the country. There is a kind of sacred respect for the earth. In India the Baiga refuse to cultivate the land with iron tools because "to open the earth's bosom" is to fail to recognize its generosity. The use of wooden tools seems less brutal. Similarly, many are convinced that man cannot change his proper destiny or the setting where he lives. . . .

Dr. Haisin, commissioned to improve the hygienic conditions of the Philippine people, had to work very hard to save rain in order to have drinkable water. The people felt that God wanted the rain to flow over the surface of the earth and if it was meant for them, they would find it in waterholes. Clearly the task of technicians encountering a mentality like this is far from easy.[3]

In India—and in general in all Eastern lands influenced by Hinduism and Buddhism, with their belief in the reincarnation of animals—a powerful obstacle to progress comes from their sacred respect for even the lowest form of life. This is because all life represents God's power and therefore should be respected. Because of reincarnation, it is possible that the soul of a man might be in an animal. And the man is paying in this way for whatever evil he committed in a previous existence. This is why Orientals are vegetarians and why destructive animals that cannot be exterminated become true scourges for agriculture. It is widely known that the cow is sacred in India (250 million cows, half of which are unproductive). Less well known is the damage caused to Indian agriculture by mice, insects of every kind, monkeys, and other animals that cannot be touched. When birds, cows, or monkeys are destroying his fields, the Indian country man beats big sticks together to make a lot of noise and chase his inopportune visitors to his neighbor's field; but he does not permit himself to kill an animal, for that would be a sacrilege. There was a real revolt of the people when the governor of India proposed a law that would allow useless or destructive animals to be killed; yet it has been calculated that between 20 and 30 percent of the grain stored in Calcutta is eaten by mice or insects. Gandhi himself, whom many consider to have been a Hindu reformer, has written:

> To me the cow is the personification of innocence. The protection of the cow is the symbol of the protection of the weak and the defenseless. . . . In my opinion the killing of cows and the killing of men are two sides of the same coin. . . . To me the cow stands for the whole subhuman world. The cow enables man to understand his identity with all that lives. . . . A Brahmin, an ant, an elephant, all belong to the same world. Hinduism insists on the brotherhood not only of all humans, but also of all living things.[4]

MAN IN WESTERN AND CHINESE ART

It is clear that no modern progress is possible as long as this idea of the relation between man and other created beings, between man and nature, prevails. And in this connection, we can best understand the different ideas that distinguish Western from non-Western culture if we contrast Western and Chinese art.

In Western culture man is *the center of all*. Not only in Christianity, but also in Graeco-Roman culture, man was considered "the masterpiece of the gods," in whom was united the beauty of nature and who stood at the center of all created things. In the West, art—the daughter of religion and the living expression of a culture—has always regarded man as the most important object of artistic representations. Man is studied in his anatomy and comportment, movements and rhythm. He is represented as the fundamental element of sculpture, painting, and every other work of art. All the rest—landscapes, plants, and animals—are decorative elements and background.

Let us now consider the art of another great civilization, such as traditional Chinese art.[5] Here we find a very different kind of mentality at work. Man is not the main focus, but only one among the many elements of nature. *The landscape is everything, man is nothing*. The three religions of China (Confucianism, Taoism, and Buddhism) seek to live in perfect harmony with nature and almost deny the presence of the human body and of human intelligence in order to turn to nature, there to lose and identify self with it. Confucius said, "A wise man finds pleasure in rivers and lakes, the virtuous in mountains." The flight from the world is the ideal of the Buddhist monk that all would like to be able to share for at least some part of one's life. Man is corrupt. He has not been redeemed as in Christianity, and the more he denies himself and his powers, the safer is his advance towards the better.

It is logical that, starting with this principle, Chinese art neglects man so that nature can be the center of his representations; because only by means of the contemplation of nature can the soul be elevated and purified. The master Wang Wei said to his students: "When depicting a landscape, allow three meters for a mountain, thirty centimeters for trees, three centimeters for horses, and three millimeters for the human figure."

Man is one of the elements of nature, a decorative element in a landscape, and nothing more. This is exactly the opposite in Western art.

In Chinese art the human figure is not studied anatomically. The nude is unknown. When a man or a woman appears in the foreground, they are caricatures rather than real persons. The human person is certainly not glorified as in the West. On the contrary, in representations of nature, mountains, trees, flowers, and animals, the Chinese artist is minutious, truly artistic, because he knows how to give life to the most insignificant detail. The Chinese also believe (or rather, formerly believed, because we are speaking of pre-Maoist China) that animals, flowers, and even mountains and rocks, have a certain degree of intelligence and feeling, and since they speak a language other than ours, we must needs silence our own human vitality in order to understand that of the creatures around us. The artist who lives in intimate contact with nature is able to use a tiny insect or even a blade of grass or the bamboo swaying in the wind for the communication of ideas. Chinese painters have understood in their mystical-symbolic language (the bamboo stands for mystical asceticism, the trunk of a tree for the vanity of material things, etc.) that they must seek the fusion of the artist with the soul of the world and nature. The human element is totally secondary; often it is missing entirely.

This study of Chinese art does not mean that it is *inferior* to Western art, but only that it is different, as different as the two cultures from which both arts are derived. It is clear that the realistic and human art of the West presupposes a whole vision of man and his relation to nature totally unlike the contemplative vision of Chinese art. It is also clear that these differences are reflected on a practical plane, with the dominion and enjoyment of nature on the one side, and its passive contemplation on the other.

It is because of cultural elements such as these that we succeed in explaining the different paths taken by different peoples and different civilizations. *Ideas move men and make history.* Buddhism, to solve the problem of suffering and evil, appeals to passive virtues, detachment from material things, suppression of all desire, and the denial of the human personality. In Islam, a derivation from the Hebrew and the Christian religions, there is a deviation to a religiosity that stresses divine providence, a form of religious fatalism that is also found in not a few uneducated Christians. Everything depends on

God's will. All man can do is to await passively the manifestations of this will and accept them. In black Africa the practice of magic is very much alive, even in modern centers and among progressive people. Natural events are attributed to the mysterious forces of nature and spirits. Man's strength therefore is for the purpose of defending himself against these malevolent powers that control him. But he makes no attempt to overcome these natural forces, only to suffer their violence. This attitude is also prevalent in popular Hinduism.

Marxists say that to bring a people to development, all sense of religion must disappear from a life, for is an alienating influence. But this is a false conclusion because true religion condemns all deviations and favors the development that gives man a sense of his own dignity as a son of God and of his superiority over all the elements and natural forces. Hebraic-Christianity points to a life diametrically opposed to that offered by other religions, one that will save man from evil and enable him to attain salvation. Man is the maker of his own destiny and with God's help he can create on earth an order of justice and peace, freeing him from the consequences of sin, injustice, oppression, and violence. It is an active, optimistic life that inspires action. It is not passive and pessimistic, nor does it lead to inaction.

STATIC CONCEPT OF THE WORLD AND OF HISTORY

As the foregoing paragraphs show, the *ideal that different civilizations propose to man are dissimilar*, as is the vision of the world and human history. In the West the human community desires to advance according to a concept of history that moves forward, towards a future which is better than the past. At least since the eruption of Christianity into the history of the West, this thrust towards a goal is very definite: to control nature, to create better living conditions for man, to preserve the freedom and dignity of the human person, to create justice among men (with equal rights and duties for all), etc. Western society is in constant progress and its march forward has brought it to the development that we know today, although this is to a large extent still incomplete.

In the third world, before contacts were made with the West—and even today among large sections of the population—the ideal is not progress, change, and advance; but preservation of the status quo, respect for traditions, and return to the customs and usages of the past. That is why the elders are so powerful and represent so massive an obstacle to progress. They control everything and can easily block every attempt at innovation initiated by young people who have received a modern education. No African or Asiatic village acts contrary to the will of the elders, the venerated guardians of tradition. How much this impedes progress can be easily imagined.

History is not seen as an advance but as a continual cyclic return to the past, a repetition of the same situations and traditions leading to no specified end. As Laloup and Nelis wrote:

> Is it necessary to repeat that religions like Brahminism and Buddhism are ahistorical? True, they acknowledge the advance of believers toward an understanding of the divine mystery and ascesis, but this is only a very weak historical perspective. If it may also be said that the doctrine of the reincarnation of the soul is in opposition and in contradistinction to all historical purpose . . . if the life of the world is an eternal circle like the seasons, if souls reincarnate themselves indefinitely in their quest for the annihilating perfection of nirvana, what dynamism, what hope can there be to continue without ceasing a life that always begins from the beginning? In Oriental religions, religious life is not conceived as a long, collective, historical journey, with a beginning, a middle, and a triumphal end.[6]

The law of the world (Karma) and the inexorable enchainment of cause and effect mean a circle without beginning or end; cyclic recurrance of the same phenomena, without any other solution than final evanescence. The Hindu story of man, like that of the Indians (and in general Orientals influenced by Hinduism and Buddhism) is well expressed in the Sastra that thus describes water:

> From the rivers that flow to the sea come the clouds,
> From the clouds come the rain and from the rain the rivers.
> This circle is also the circle of Karma.
> From the beginning of the world until the end of all suffering.

Nehru, explaining why India is underdeveloped, blamed English colonialism (very serious as we shall see in the next chapter), but then added that the fundamental cause is the difference between the Indian and European mind:

> This is the vital question. In Europe invisible forces seethe within the masses, leading to continual development. In India, on the contrary, the situation is static. . . . The static nature of Indian society refuses to evolve in a world in evolution.[7]

Also in Africa (let us repeat, in traditional African society) the general mentality is antiprogressive, without any idea of progress; the purpose of man and society is not to go forward but to preserve and to revive old traditions. Hamidou Kane, an African student, writes:

> The most serious of all the internal defects of African society seems to me to be the ignorance of our culture about progress. It is also possible that this idea may be an original European creation and the reason for its technical triumph. This idea is not known here. The past, a mythic and divine past, determines our culture. A friend said to me the other day: "We are making our progress in our past."[8]

Alioune Diop, director of Présence Africaine, and organizer of a congress of men of African culture, wrote:

> Notions of progress, revolution, and change are specifically European. Neither China nor the black world can rationally justify change.[9]

Another African student, Dr. S. B. Kouyaté, writing about the politics of development in Africa, declared:

> The modernization of agriculture is not only a technical problem but above all a human psychological problem, because it seeks to make a true revolution in the rural African world. There is need to acquire this sensitivity to progress, this tendency towards a higher life—in a word, the will to leave misery. The basic problem then is psychological.[10]

In Japan during the last century, when contact with the West was established, it was found that even the word "revolution" was unknown. A change of any kind was expressed by the Confucian phrase "a modification in the dispositions of heaven." Japan developed rapidly under the rule of a military dictatorship, thanks to Emperor Meiji's enforced imposition of Western laws and education. But at the middle of the last century, prior to contact with the West, society was tightly closed, rigidly divided into castes and classes,[11] without any idea of progress, and living only in the worship of tradition. Throughout the whole of Japanese history there was never any sign of an internal drive towards social revolution, democracy, and social justice. Nor was this a traditional goal in literature and philosophy, even though the existing feudal system was already a forerunner of modern society.[12]

The development of Japan in the course of the last century plainly shows that the third world is capable of developing in the same way. All men are equal. All racism is false. Everything depends on "the revolution of ideas" that most of the third world has not yet experienced. We see, for instance, the restraining power that prejudices and traditions exercise over development. In many parts of the third world, the principal obstacle to the modernization of agriculture is not the lack of technicians or the means (even though they be limited), but the inability to persuade the people to change their methods of cultivation, to introduce new crops, to use artificial irrigation, to vary their diet, etc. Dietary prejudices are well known to students of hunger and malnutrition. Some peoples are suffering from malnutrition only because they are not using the food that is already available. For example, the Peuls, an African tribe of pastoral people, eat meat only at sacrificial rites. This is not because they do not like meat or because there is not enough, but because the Peuls look upon animals as man's friends and allow them to die a natural death without using them as food.

The same is true throughout the East in lands of Hindu or Buddhist culture. As a general rule, people do not eat meat, only agricultural products and fish—again, not because animals are lacking or because they could not be raised, but because it is not the custom to eat meat or animal products (milk, eggs, cheese, etc). To be sure, delicacies of our Western diet include very good dishes made without meat. But if one eats only rice, a few greens, or dried fish for a whole life, the result is serious malnutrition. Yet deeply rooted prejudices are not easily changed in a static society with rigid structures.

A DIFFERENT CONCEPT OF WORK

Besides "the revolution of ideas," the third world lacks the revolution of science and technology. The reason for this is easily explained. Having no idea of man's dignity or any concept of progress, the relation between man and nature becomes one of contemplation, not of tension, discovery, and conquest on man's part. In the same way, work is looked upon purely as a means of subsistence, not an instrument for the improvement of one's own condition and of the whole of society. When there is nothing to eat, one works; when there is enough to eat, work is unnecessary. In other words, to produce more than one consumes, to save, to improve one's own position for the sake of tomorrow—this was something which African and traditional Asiatic society did not know.

Some peoples who found subsistence difficult because of the aridity of the soil, worked earnestly and constructed great irrigation systems—as did the ancient Egyptians, for example, at the time they built the pyramids. But this undertaking contributed nothing to society's progress. It gave no stimulus to social revolution because it was not the result of the revolution of ideas, but merely a means for survival. The same may be said of China's scientific achievements of the past: the compass, the map, gunpowder, advances in astronomy and mathematics. None of these had any influence on the general evolution of Chinese society, but remained isolated within the whole static situation of the great empire; they could not be used for progress because society had not experienced "the revolution of ideas."

Many white people who travel around Africa say: "The blacks do not want to work." This is not true. It is not that they do not want to work, only that they have a different idea of work. They do not have a drive to work. They do not live in a money economy (so it is not possible for them to save). Work is considered only as a means of survival, not as a way of controlling nature and improving one's standard of life.

Noel Drogat relates this incident:

A few years ago a young, enterprising missionary sent to Europe for some plows with metal plowshares to be used for increasing the rice harvest, and then taught the peasants how to use them.

Though plowing was not done without fatigue, because the oxen were not accustomed to so much effort, the harvest was good, and quantity of rice was doubled. But when it came time for the second sowing of the year the missionary was amazed to see no one working in the rice fields. "Why is nothing being done?" he asked. "Are you going to allow your rice fields to remain uncultivated?" The answer was simple: "We have harvested enough rice for a whole year, why work any more? But do not be troubled, next year we shall sow rice again."

These words express all the indolence and fatalism of these people. Accustomed as they are to living on very little, at a subsistence level, they see no need for doing any more than is necessary to obtain the minimum food indispensable to life. [13]

Work and the whole economic idea of society depends on the idea of life that the people hold. Where there is no idea of progress or improvement in the standard of living, there is no effort toward advancement or foresight for tomorrow. Dr. Louis-Paul Aujoulat spoke of the exorbitant expenses incurred by Africans at the times of funerals and marriages: unproductive outlays that cannot be paid for during a lifetime. We Westerners consider this to be madness, while the Africans in their nonprogressive culture see no other way to live and spend. [14]

The fundamental problem of development, therefore, involves education in new concepts of life, the development of a new mentality and culture. Albert Hirschmann writes about the countries of the third world:

Some suppose that if we were to eliminate one or more obstacles to progress, the forces proper to development itself would rush forward like racehorses when the stall doors are opened. My experience leads me to doubt the existence of progressive energy that could be restrained by oppressive measures. I hold that it is precisely this inability to make decisions about development that accounts for all the other difficulties of underdeveloped countries. [15]

H. Desroche, another development expert, writes:

It is normal in the traditionalist societies [of Africa] to find not the will to development but indifference to development. [16]

THE DISTANCE BETWEEN A DYNAMIC MENTALITY AND A STATIC ONE

Anyone who has visited the third world, particularly rural regions where local traditions have not yet begun to be changed by modern ideas of life, can see for himself the distance that separates Western mentality—that tends to progress spontaneously—from the mentality of men for whom progress has no meaning. I will cite some facts reported by eyewitnesses in various underdeveloped countries.

In India I visited a pariah village during the busy rice-harvesting season. The village was filled with chattering men and women. I asked the missionary, who knew these people well and spoke their language, why they were not working on a day when they could earn a good bit of money. He answered that a buffalo had died during the night and the people were all going to eat it.

In Manaos in Brazilian Amazonia, at the time I visited there in 1966, fruit and fresh vegetables were brought—by air, of course —from São Paulo in southern Brazil, a distance of two thousand miles. Imagine the price of an orange or an apple. From Manaos I went to some villages on the right bank of the Amazon. They were in the highlands, safe from the inundations of the great river, and consequently able to produce fruit and vegetables as the Japanese were beginning to do not far away. In the villages where Indians and *caboclos* (settlers) were living, only fish and manioca were eaten. I saw some orange trees growing near the cabins, and asked the people why they did not raise large quantities of oranges and sell them in Manaos, since the money they would make would enable them to build stone houses and live a more human life. No matter how often I talked to young and older men, I never succeeded in making them understand this concept that seemed so obvious to me. Their invariable answer was: "We already eat all the oranges we want."

Situations like this may seem absurd, isolated, atypical cases, yet they correspond exactly to a mentality very common in the third world where the people lack "an anxiety about progress" that we in our turn possess to an exaggerated degree. To give another example, in Tanzania corn is a basic staple. Now the kind of corn traditionally raised there gave a low yield, and government officials have tried to introduce a hybrid corn with a yield four or five times greater. They have had little success. The people have confidence in their own corn and do not want anything new. They are not accustomed to see corn grow so tall (about nine feet instead of twenty to thirty inches), and they say they like what they have. At Iringa, in the south of Tanzania, a government technician told me that if he succeeded in having the selected seeds sown, there would be a superabundant production of corn that would give better nourishment to men and animals, and make the land more productive and exports possible. Yet the people are slow to accept it. The missionaries have been asked by the government to do some propagandizing, in order to get the people to use the new corn seed.

An anxiety about progress enables the individual and the group to accept novelty, whether technical, social, or cultural. Conversely, those who live in a purely subsistence economy have no aspirations beyond day-to-day living. They lack a mentality open to progress. They do not want change or novelty because they do not see any use in them. Instead of turning to the future, they turn to the past; instead of going forward, they prefer to stand still and preserve the status quo.

When an entire people or social group (tribe, clan, or village) is imprisoned in this traditional mentality, it is difficult even for the single individual to escape. I remember, in many parts of Africa, being told of cases like the following. A young man of more developed mentality, full of goodwill, set about raising a new crop. His efforts were successful, and he began to sell the fruits of his labor, making a little money. Instead of encouraging others to emulate him, his success suddenly became a source of trouble. Jealousy was aroused, and the elders condemned his actions. His relations flocked to him with endless demands, while the villagers and tribesmen avoided him as if he were an apostate, or else asked impossible things of him. If this boy had been in a small town that was developing, he might somehow have managed to get ahead; however, he lives in a rural region where tradition reigns, and sooner or later he will be forced to submit and return to a subsistence economy. At least then he will have a little peace.

CONCRETE CASES SEEN IN AFRICA

The "laziness," then, of which the whites in Africa accuse the natives, is not laziness in our sense of the word, but a passivity and lack of initiative that are, even for the courageous, the results of suffocating surroundings.

Yet laziness has other origins. Sometimes, as we have said, it is related to a concept of work different from our own. In many parts of Africa, for example, field laborers are on a level with women. This is a tradition that is respected, and no one would allow himself to fail in respect. Among the Karamojon of Uganda, women age very quickly because of childbearing and hard work in the fields. The building of cabins and the cultivation of the soil are also reserved for women. Taking care of animals and carrying water (to fill a bucket they sometimes have to go for miles on foot) are the work of children and young boys and girls. Men, on the contrary, lead an easy life. They spend long hours talking, watching their families work, smoking tobacco, stealing animals, and making forays against neighboring tribes. Their work never goes further than some trifling shopkeeping, woodcarving, basketweaving, skintanning, or metalworking to produce spears and small knives.

Karamojon men are tall, straight, athletic, imposing figures. Their women, on the contrary, poor beasts of burden, are ugly to look at after their first youth. The emancipation of women is still to come. To a woman who may complain—a very rare occurrence—the husband answers, "Do you not know that I paid 40 cows for you?" The problem of the heavy dowry that the man must pay to the bride's family is another tradition that is a great obstacle to progress.

With a simple piece of material over his shoulders, or sometimes wholly naked, and a spear and a wooden shield in his hand, the male Karamojon feels that he is king of the arid and parched land of Karamoja. He has held himself aloof from the conquerors, and even when he asks a coin from the tourist who wishes to take his picture, he does so with an imperious tone that brooks no refusal. He is the depository of tribal wisdom, and the master of all the beasts and people in his house. He always has someone to wait on him. When there is famine, the man is always the last to suffer because he is always the first to eat. In a situation like that why would a Karamojon man want to make any change? Modern progress means nothing to him. He is very well off just as he is.[17]

The Karamaojon of Uganda are perfect examples of the precolonial period, before revolutionary ideas and military conquests changed local society. But many Africans are already more evolved and have overcome certain obstacles to development proper to more primitive peoples only to encounter others that are no less serious. This seems to me to be the first: that the evolved African despises manual labor, and will not "debase" himself to cultivate the land or to do any other work he considers servile. In Africa anyone who has finished the fifth grade of elementary schooling aspires to a position in the administration of the state or to become a teacher or politician. That is why the towns are filled with unemployed intellectuals who live by means of a thousand jobs and expedients (taxi drivers, photographers, runners, servants, porters, etc.), but feel no drive to become industrial entrepreneurs, superintendents, or modern farmers.

In Kapala I came to know Joseph Odinko very well, a twenty-year-old taxi driver who has spent a few years in the seminary. I made a long trip in his taxi from Kapala to Goma in the Congo, across the southern part of Uganda. We were together in his car for four days, and I was able to discuss many subjects with this boy who spoke good English as well as several local languages. He had exceptional physical powers (he was able to withstand fatigue, had great muscular strength, etc.).

Though appreciative of Joseph's fine human qualities, I must say that what I most admired and never ceased to marvel at was his intelligence. Yet his highest ambition was to become a state employee, and he spoke disdainfully of all manual or agricultural work. When I tried to explain to him that perhaps with his gifts he could begin some productive activity of his own, artisan or industrial, I might just as well have been talking to a Martian, for those ambitions had never entered his mind. In fact, his approach to life was passive, not active. A young white man, having the same qualities as Joseph, would have had an entirely different mentality.

OPINIONS FROM THE THIRD WORLD

In the Declaration of Arusha, the basic document of socialism in Tanzania, we read:

The essential condition for development is hard work. Everyone wants progress, but all do not understand or accept the foundations that development requires. The basic requisite is hard work. Let us go into the villages and talk to our people to find out if it is possible or not for them to work harder.[18]

The text continues to affirm that under modern conditions in the city the work week is forty-five hours, with a maximum of four weeks' vacation during the year.

It would be interesting to ask our country people, especially the men, how many hours a week they work, and for how many weeks of the year. Many work only half the time, for which they accept payment. The truth is that the women in the villages work very hard. . . . But the men in the villages (and some city women) rest for almost half their lives. The energies of millions of men in the villages and of millions of women in the city that today are being wasted in chattering, dancing, and drinking are a great treasure that could contribute much to the country's development.

The phenomenon of "social parasitism" that President Jomo Kenyatta of Kenya denounced in his address comes from this concept of work as merely a means of subsistence. If a person works in the city and earns a wage, his relatives and friends come from the village to be supported by him. The sense of solidarity among the members of a family or clan is undoubtedly positive, but it becomes negative when one of the family members becomes part of the modern economy. This also explains why those who are able to earn a little more, or able to engage in some economic activity, sometimes give up the idea lest they be working for others.

I remember while having tea with a high official of the Ministry of Education in Kampala in Uganda, I asked him what was the monthly wage. He answered: "Oh, Father, the more we raise the wage, the greater the number of relatives who have to be supported."

Kenyatta writes in a recent book:

Many people in good health and able to work come to the city and spend many months living at the expense of family and friends. They are a true plague. . . . This is a real waste of manpower. . . . These people, well able to work, exploit their relatives and friends, and are a disgrace to themselves and to our society. Their relations and friends ought to free themselves from these people and refuse to give them anything to eat.[19]

If we move from Africa to Asia it is more difficult to generalize because of the complexity of the Asian continent. The concept of work acts as the obstacle to development of peoples of certain mentalities and the social structures closely resemble those of Africa. Speaking of the rural sections in the Philippines, an observer, attempting to explain the slow socioeconomic growth, said:

> Anyone who takes any initiative outside his own family group becomes inflated with pride and the last thing that a Filipino can think of is to break with his own family. A man was persuaded to build in his own field a small irrigation system that tripled his production of rice. But he had to give it up, because his family came at once to "borrow" rice from him now that he was rich. Consequently, he had less rice in the end than he had had before. "How can I insist on maturity," the director of the Rural Bank of Taguig said to me, "when I give loans to my aunts, my cronies, my cousins . . . ?" Also, when an individual does not want to work, it never occurs to anyone to drive him from the house. On the other hand, the disadvantages of this system of family solidarity are fully balanced by the atmosphere of mutual understanding and devotion that makes life more bearable.[20]

The low level of the Indian's productivity, as that of other Asian peoples, is strongly conditioned by malnutrition and an enervating climate. There is also the weight of Indian tradition of which the Indian sociologist, A. Parel, writes:

> Within the limits of a generalization, it may be said that according to Indian tradition manual work was considered socially inferior. There was a vast difference between the man who worked with his hands and the man who used his head. Until recent times the Indian was not concerned with economic problems; he devoted himself to mysticism, literature, mythology. The intellectual left trade, industry, and agriculture to those thought to be incapable of any form of intellectual life. Economic activity stagnated; it was the mere repetition of a tradition. Thus rational intelligence was not applied to practical problems.[21]

The Indian ambassador to Paris, K. M. Panikkar, wrote in a book devoted to the problems of new states:

In India, education, with its long tradition of humane studies, offers no stimulus to work. The Chinese mandarin, it is said, allowed their nails to grow very long to show their aversion to work. In fact the man of Eastern lands had in general adopted an attitude of disdain in regard to manual work.[22]

Another Indian sociologist, P. Thomas, wrote in a recent book:

It must be admitted that in general the Indian of our day admires passivity more than activity. To most Indians inaction seems to be a kind of spiritual excellence. . . . It must be admitted that the Hindu attitude to life is more or less philosophic. Granted that pessimism is the dominant note of his philosophy, the Hindu considers suffering to be a necessary condition of life, and therefore shows less impatience then his Western brother in the presence of misfortunes. This has brought the Hindu to a fatal reconciliation with every form of suffering and made him less eager to improve social and political conditions than would be the Westerner. . . . Upper Indian classes indulge in gluttony and avoid any work that requires the use of physical energy. A Hindu who has enough money to support himself and his family thinks that it would be degrading to do any kind of manual work.[23]

Thomas says that the Hindu habitually "speaks of his own culture as essentially spiritual, and considers the success of Western nations as purely materialistic," adding that his way of thinking reflects "an inferiority complex." Nehru, in his *Autobiography*, said the same thing:

It is common knowledge (in India) that in the modern, industrial West external development has notably surpassed inner development but it does not follow, as many Easterners seem to imagine, that while perhaps we are industrially retarded and our exterior development is slow, our inner evolution is superior. This is one of the illusions with which we try to comfort ourselves and overcome our inferiority complex.[24]

POSITIVE VALUES TO BE PRESERVED IN AFRO-ASIAN CULTURES

What we have been saying about Africans and Asiatics could seem excessively critical—to some it may even seem to be racist. But we do not say that the people of the third world are constitutionally incapable of raising themselves; on the contrary, we have returned from our travels in Asia and Africa with a feeling of optimism about the future of these people, for we have observed an exceptional human quality that should be an example for us in the West. However, this is a study of the reasons why the third world is not developed and what internal causes have held it in a static state until our own day. As we have said above, it seems to us that the principal causes are cultural, human, psychological, and a question of mentality.

If we accept the hypothesis, illustrated in the preceding chapter, that the dynamic culture of the Western people comes from no racial superiority over other people but from the revolution of ideas generated by the biblical-Christian message (that there was an eruption of God in the history of man), then we see that the search ends in a nonethnic way. The progress of the West, not only scientific-technical and economic but also social, is valid in its content, but not in its various historic forms, for all people. In other words, it is valid as an incentive to betterment, to social justice, to respect for human dignity, and to the better use of nature, not in the concrete form in which it is expressed—that is, in the various forms of the organization of production and of society (capitalism, Marxism, exploitation of man, etc.). It is valid, I repeat, in its basic idea in a drive towards a better world, because it is based on divine revelation and not on particular human intuitions. It is the common patrimony of mankind that the West has realized first only because it was the first to receive God's message for all men.

Today it cannot be denied that the third world is being Westernized, and this seems to be a positive fact in the sense that soon every culture will be penetrated by the revolution of ideas that historically was embodied in the West—not because of Western genius, but because of the word of God that penetrated and transformed the West's culture. However, the Westernization of the third world is not a positive but a negative fact, if by "Westernization" is meant that other peoples should imitate the materialistic pattern of the West and our inhuman ways of organizing society (for example, capitalism and Marxism, to say nothing of the various kinds of fascism and racism).

Non-Western cultures, therefore, are not inferior or negative or surpassed. They are simply cultures elaborated by man without the light of divine revelation but with a great many positive human qualities that Asians and Africans ought to safeguard in their advance towards an integral human development: joy in life, optimism, serenity, hospitality, and tolerance, to list but a few. In Africa, even in villages where life still follows the traditional pattern, I have often noticed that there is a feeling of benevolent solidarity among the people which we in the West do not have. A missionary from Tanzania said to me: "In our villages the spirit of benevolent help is spontaneous and has a depth difficult to imagine in Europe. If a man is sick, everyone goes to work on his land—no need to ask anyone, they all act spontaneously. If there is a misfortune in a family, help is quickly given. If children are left alone, they are soon received into another house and treated as members of the family, without a thought that this is anything out of the ordinary."

This solidarity among the members of a tribe or village is a value that we Westerners have lost and that Africans should try to maintain—but within fair limits, so as to avoid the social parasitism of which we previously spoke above. In India the nonviolence, the tolerance, the respect for another's conduct (even when it is bizarre), are virtues innate in the people. Perhaps in no other country in the world is there such freedom of thought and action as in India. It is rare to see an Indian scream or otherwise lose his calm. His patience and his spirit of adaptation, like his sense of nonviolence, are inherent.

The people of the third world are not moving along a path of decadence, some symptoms of which can be seen in our Western society: escapism through drugs, the trend toward anarchy and violence, pansexualism, etc. They are a young people who have not to this point crossed the threshold of modern progress, for they are still prisoners of a pretechnical mentality. They have not yet acquired the anxiety of development that is a characteristic of a developed people and is the first cause of development itself. In this there is no moral fault. It would be absurd to accuse Africans and Asiatics of being what they are because their societies have difficulty in developing as a result of local, historical, and cultural factors, particularly since we imperialists are largely responsible for their condition, as we shall see in the following chapter. Each people has its own history, and Italy, for example, feels in no way inferior to Sweden simply because it has not achieved the same extent of industrialization and modern organization.

A LOOK AT INADEQUATE SOCIAL STRUCTURES

The discussion of the internal causes of underdevelopment in the countries of the third world could be lengthened by many more pages, especially in regard to the inadequate social structures that arrest the dynamism required to establish a society in the modern sense. I will limit myself to a few.[25]

In Africa tribalism creates divisions within the countries and appears in politics where parties have a tribal basis and minority tribes are oppressed. In his address to the Kenyan nation, President Kenyatta went so far as to castigate tribal rivalry as "the cancer of our country." In almost all the countries of black Africa "unity" is a magic word like "Africanization," because it expresses a deeply felt need. To go to Africa for only a little while and to live in close contact with the people is to realize the extent of tribalism and racial strife as formidable obstacles to progress.

To us Westerners the Africans are generically "black," just as we are "white" to them; yet the differences between the different ethnic groups and tribes are more marked than are these distinctions. At first sight it is difficult for us to distinguish an Italian from a Frenchman, a German from a Spaniard. True, different nationalities have different characteristics, but these are not always valid —an Italian may be blond, a German brunette. In the regions of Africa that I visited, after a few days in one place it was fairly easy for me, after the characteristic signs had been explained (skin color, facial features, ornaments, clothes, etc.) to distinguish the members of the different tribes and local races. To these externals should be added diversity in language, rites and traditions, mentality, and in some cases, religions. Also, not so long ago, and in some places even today, there were conflicts over game, land, water, and the like, that made for further divisions among the people.

In the future, as has happened in the West, the establishment of a unifying language, intermarriage, and relocation of people for reasons of work will gradually lead to the disappearance of ethnic differences and the formation of united countries. But for the moment the great majority of African nations are still divided entities, created around conference tables or by the conquests of colonial troops, and not yet a deep experience for the people who live there. The fact is that Kenya (or any other country) has to make its people Kenyans because now there are only Kikuyus, Luos, Merus, Kambras, Boranas, and others. Some Kenyans do not even know that there is a state called Kenya.

What is the consequence of this still-incomplete formation of spirit and national identity? This above all: that contrasting tribal traditions are brought into politics and are more divisive than are our political parties and social classes. In our countries a Fascist can become a Communist without too much trouble, or a laborer an entrepreneur; but in Kenya a Kikuyu can never become a Meru. Political parties in general represent different tribes and different regional interests, so it is easy to understand why a representative of a given tribe in an administrative position on any level means the advancement of the members of that tribe and of no other. If a member of a certain tribe were to be entrusted with the supervision of a local railroad, very soon all the workers on that railroad would be members of the supervisor's tribe; all others would have to seek jobs elsewhere.

The advancement of one tribe or race at the cost of the oppression of the others is why Indians are not highly regarded throughout East Africa. The Indians control certain areas of the economy and local administration (trade, restaurants, railroads, etc.) and access to them by others is impossible.

The recent expulsion of Asians from Uganda, for example, shows that this is not to be tolerated when it is done by foreigners, such as the Indians now, or whites in times past; but it has to be accepted when it is a question of a local race. If the Kikuyu in Kenya, the Baganda in Uganda, the Amhara in Ethiopia, and the Arabs of the Sudan assume control of the state, they advance their own race, reserving for themselves the better positions, schools, state finances, etc.; as a result the other races and tribes are crushed. This is inevitable because the minority races and those less developed have to submit to laws promulgated by the stronger. Their only escape is to rebel, as did the south Sudanese Negroes and the Eritrei. Hope of success is slim.

The investigation that we have made somewhat in depth of tribalism in Africa could be repeated for many other internal social causes of the underdevelopment of the third world, but we would run the risk of making this an interminably long chapter. Let us limit ourselves to a few examples, keeping always in mind that the description of inadequate social structures is not meant to be an accusation of the people of the third world, much less a kind of racism or an implication that they are an inferior people. Nothing could be further from my convictions. We are simply speaking of a culture and a society that are related to the modern world not by internal desire but by external influences; consequently these people find themselves unprepared for this leap across centuries and millenia, and for the assimilation in a short space of time of ideas and concepts of a totally new life. It is little wonder, then, that the structures of this society are behind the times, even though today they are being rapidly updated.

In India, the rigid caste divisions, especially in rural areas, are, as Nehru has strongly stated, "the most serious obstacle to our development." These divisions continue to exist, even after state law has abolished them, because they are deeply rooted in Indian culture and traditions. Polygamy, feudal structures, large landholdings (which is particularly serious in Latin America), the lack of political maturity which leads to a dictatorial form of government—all these are obstacles to development. In third-world countries one is aware of the absence of a dynamic middle class able to represent what the bourgeoisie has historically represented in the economic development of the West. Everywhere in Asia, Africa, Latin America, and also in underdeveloped areas of Europe (for example, in not-yet-developed southern Italy), the distance that separates the few rich from the very many poor is abysmal in every aspect of life: money, culture, political power, material benefits, etc. Such a social structure naturally tends to preserve the status quo, to remain unchanged. The few rich people have no interest, and some have no idea, as to how changes might be made; while the many poor are too depressed, too unaware, and too lacking in capacity and training to be able to change. The social situation of the third world is precisely this: immobility due to the absence of an inner drive toward development. Yves Lacoste, has written:

Today many underdeveloped lands outside of Europe are living as if this were the eighteenth century. They are brilliant but immobile. Unlike the countries of Western Europe they possess no social group able to initiate their own transformation and to destroy their internal chains. . . . This is not due to external causes or to any technical backwardness, but essentially to internal structural causes.[26]

Barbara Ward concludes her historical examination of the evolution of the third world with these words:

In short, the chief point that distinguishes tribal and traditional society is that all the internal impulses to modernization have been largely lacking. And yet today these societies are everywhere in a ferment of change. How has this come about? Where did the external stimulus come from? There is only one answer. It came, largely uninvited, from the restless, changing, rampaging West. In the last three hundred years, the world's ancient societies, the great traditional civilizations of the East, together with the pre-Columbian civilizations of Latin America and the tribal societies of Africa, have all, in one way or another, been stirred up from outside by the new, bounding, uncontrollable energies of the Western powers which, during these same years, were undergoing concurrently all the revolutions—of equality, of nationalism, of rising population, and of scientific change—which make up the mutation of modernization. The great world-wide transmitter of the modernizing tendency has been without doubt—for good and evil—Western colonialism.[27]

FOOTNOTES

1. Contempt for men of other races and cultures is more or less common in all peoples. In the sixteenth century the Japanese called the Europeans barbarians because they did not bathe every day and ate with their hands.

2. In *Nigrizia*, Verona, October 1969, p. 12.

3. *I paesi della fame*, E.M.I., Milan, 1964, pp. 60-61.

4. Quoted by A. Parel in *L'Osservatore Romano*, April 8, 1966, p. 2.

5. We speak of traditional Chinese art because today, under the Maoist regime, art in China has adopted all the "realistic" values of communism and man is now central in every artistic representation.

6. *Culture et Civilisation*, pp. 161-162.

7. *The Discovery of India*, ed. Robert I. Crane, New York, Doubleday Anchor Books, 1960, p. 283.

8. "Comme si nous étions donné rendez-vous," *Espirit*, Paris, October 1961, p. 382.

9. Quoted in E. Toaldo, "Fattori culturali e politici dello sviluppo," in *Primo corso studi terzo mondo*, PIME, Milan, 1969, n. 6, p. 7

10. Kouyaté, S. B., *Politiques du développement et voies africaines su socialisme*, "Présence Africaine," 1963, n. 47, p. 60.

11. Even today in Japan there are two or three million "eta," the first inhabitants of the archipelago who were integrated with the Japanese, yet remained in the margin of society, in a closed caste, in part economically underdeveloped.

12. Notice that even among the ancient Greeks who were rational and pragmatic, history had no meaning. There was no messianic hope. No fulfillment of history was awaited. There was nothing worth looking forward to, nothing worth fighting for.

13. *Op. cit.*, pp. 47-48.

14. *Action sociale et développement*, pp. 93-94.

15. A. O. Hirschman, *The Strategy of Economic Development*, New Haven, Conn., Yale University Press, 1958, p. 25.

16. "Aspects du système coopératif en milieu rural africain." Communication made to the Economic Conference of Africa and Malaga, April 16, 1964, at Marseille.

17. Anyone who wants further information about the Karamojon whom we have described so briefly should consult: F. Farina, *Nel paese dei bevitori di sangue*, Nigrizia, Bologna, 1965.

18. Original text in Julius K. Nyerere, *Freedom and Socialism*, Oxford University Press, Dar Es Salaam, 1969, pp. 244-245.

19. *Suffering Without Bitterness*, East African Publishing House, Nairobi, 1968, pp. 233-234.

20. G. Melis, "Riso e guistizia nelle campagne delle Filippine," in *Civiltà Catholica*, May 4, 1968, p. 242.

21. La "malattia dell'India" in *L'Osservatore Romano*, April 3, 1966.

22. *Problèmes des Etats nouveaux*, Calmann-Lévy, Paris, 1959, p. 93.

23. *Hindu Religion, Customs, and Manners*, Taraporevala Sons, Bombay, 1960, pp. 129-130.

24. Feltrinelli, Milan, 1955, p. 391.

25. To go more deeply into the internal çauses of underdevelopment in the third world, see Chapter 4, "Strutture sociali oppressive e paralizzanti" (pp. 78-125) of Y. Lacoste's *Geografia del sottosviluppo*.

26. *Les pays sous-développés*, P.U.F., Paris, 1966, p. 53.

27. *The Rich Nations and the Poor Nations*, p. 51.

THE AMBIGUITY
OF THE EXTERNAL
CAUSES OF
UNDERDEVELOPMENT

4

Until recently many underdeveloped countries were—and some still are—colonies of more economically advanced countries. Today, although the majority of these lands have achieved political independence, they find themselves still subject to "the law of the stronger," that is, they are victims of the so-called economic neocolonialism. The effect of these two phenomena (colonialism and neocolonialism) on the development of the third world is not understood in the same way by all scholars. In the past, during the colonial period, there was a tendency to exalt the benefits and the "civilization" that colonization brought to primitive countries, and ignore or minimize the serious damage done to that society and its economy. Today the opposite attitude prevails. Western countries, as the result of their interventions in the third world, are held responsible for famine and underdevelopment.

These two interpretations, contradictory and prejudiced, do not correspond fully to the facts, which are far more complex. In the preceding chapter we have already given examples of the internal causes of socioeconomic stagnation that have kept the third world underdeveloped, especially the cultural causes that are at the base of a given civilization and account for its development in one way rather than in another. But the explanation is not complete. In addition to the internal causes originating in the countries of the third world, there are others that are external—for example, the interference of the West in the economy of underdeveloped societies that in past times was accompanied by military occupation (colonialism), and today manifests itself through economic and political imperialism (neocolonialism).

We believe that colonialism and neocolonialism are in themselves ambivalent in regard to the development of the third world: in certain aspects they are negative, in certain others they are positive. Whether the negative elements outweigh the positive, or vise versa, admits of no easy generalization. Each country must be studied by itself in the light of its past history and present situation. Here it will suffice to examine the complexity of colonialism and neocolonialism, on the one hand, in order to see the very grave responsibility of the West in relation to poor people, and on the other to show that the underdevelopment of the third world is not due solely to causes external to the third world itself. This analysis will enable us to trace the lines of our commitment as Western Christians to the struggle against hunger and want.

NEGATIVE ASPECTS OF COLONIALISM

We now intend to examine the negative effects of historical colonialism that today have nearly disappeared in the development of the third world. Here we are referring to Western colonization, begun in the fifteenth century (with the Portuguese and Spanish geographical discoveries), without denying (we say this incidentally) that there is also an Arab colonization of the Negro-African peoples and many other oppressive forms of colonization among the people of the third world itself. But our discussion will be limited to European colonization, justly accused of being the cause of many of the ills that even today plague former colonies.

First of all, it should be said that colonization is based on the *principle of the advantage to the mother country.* The interests of the colonizing country enjoyed an absolute priority over those of the colonized people. Only much later, through the League of Nations after the First World War, and the United Nations after the Second, was the principle admitted, at least theoretically, that the colonial power should lead its colonies towards economic and political maturity so that they would be able to rule themselves. But for many centuries—and also in our own, but with opposing declarations of principle—the essential purpose of colonization was not so much the economic and social elevation of the poor as the exploitation of lands overseas for the benefit of the conquering nations. So true is this that the only lands that were colonized were those that had something of immediate interest—mineral, agricultural, or commercial—to offer to the mother country. The others were left alone. No wonder that, starting from principles of this kind, colonization gravely damaged the third world. We shall see what these harmful effects were:

(a) *Rupture in the balance of economic subsistence.* Traditional society of the third world produced little but also increased little in population. So a natural equilibrium was established between production and population. Men died easily, whether through infant mortality (more than 50 percent of the babies died before they were a year old), or deaths due to tribal wars, recurring famines, epidemics, floods, and other causes.

The introduction of modern medicine and the establishment of social peace brought about a rapid population explosion, while agricultural production remained more or less the same or was orientated by the colonizing powers toward the production of things highly valued for exportation to the neglect of food production for the populace.

At the beginning of our century the population of the Philippines was almost the same as that of Belgium—about seven million people. Today there are eleven million people in Belgium, but in the Philippines there are thirty-six million. The same phenomenon can more or less be observed in the other third-world countries. The introduction of Western medicine literally revolutionized their biological rhythm and brought about a population growth far higher than that of Europe or North America, without in any way bringing with it the capacity for economic development.

Let this be made clear. It unquestionably was good to lower the rate of infant mortality, but at the same time the colonial powers made no attempt to increase production or to lead colonized lands to industrialization and modern agricultural methods. Medical men, economists, and politicians did not coordinate their efforts; consequently today in the third world we have a rapidly increasing population and a production that is static or advancing weakly. According to some authorities, Dumont for example, this is the basic characteristic of underdevelopment.

Concrete data for India clearly show the long period of stagnation that agricultural production underwent during the years of English colonization and the rapidity with which the population increased. After independence, that is, from 1947 until today, the population continued to increase, but agricultural production also moved forward.

Year	Inhabitants (millions)	Annual production of grain (millions of tons)
1870	180	50
1947	380	62
1969	530	110

The responsibility of the colonial powers on the nutritional level is very serious, and it can be said that their unenlightened interventions created the tragic food problems of their former colonies. This does not mean, as some think, that before colonization there was no hunger in Asia or in Africa. There was. Yet it took the form of a seasonal dearth, not a chronic absence of food for large numbers of the people.

(b) *Rupture in the psychological-social and cultural balance.* Before colonization, the society of the third world enjoyed a culture, stability, and psychological tranquility that it lost in its violent contact with the Western world. A culture for which they were not prepared was imposed on them, the old culture and social systems were imperiled, and nothing of greater value was introduced.

The enthusiasm of some who write about the old Asian or African world is undoubtedly too romantic to be credible. It was a cruel society. The law of the stronger prevailed. The weak were oppressed without mercy. Take, for example, the despotic power of man over woman, of larger races and tribes over smaller ones, of sultans and heads of tribes over their subordinates. Nevertheless it was a society with an inner cohesion, one that was able to give life a certain security. The violent impact of Western culture weakened old institutions at their roots and wrenched the non-Western peoples from their past, imposing values of another civilization but allowing no time for a gradual adjustment. It is difficult for us to imagine what all this means: the collapse of a whole vision of life, of all beliefs, of every authority, the loss for a people of their identity; all this makes man listless, without energy, "melancholic," continuously regretting a past world that will never come back. We should not imagine a "melancholy" as we know it when we are far from home; it is a question instead of a deep feeling which may even lead to a premature death.

Another reaction which has been observed among the most "primitive" people of the third world, when they are in contact with Western culture, is a tendency toward "prophetic, salvation-bringing" movements, such as those messianic sects which promise the people a miraculous salvation under the guidance of a charismatic leader, who sums up all the qualities of his race and of local traditions and who throws himself against white oppressors. This phenomenon has been studied by ethnologists, including Italians, who reveal to us, Western men, the degree of violence that white colonization has engendered. These "messianic, salvation-bringing" sects are very widespread in black Africa, often in the form of "African Churches," and in other regions inhabited by peoples without writing (New Guinea, tribal population of Asia, American Indians, etc.).[1]

The crumbling of the psychological balance has created in the third world "an inferiority complex," more or less pronounced (in accordance with the positions and the degree of culture or the characteristics of various persons) toward the white man; and this fact hampers the ordered development of local cultures. This inferiority complex increased by racism and "slavism" stems from the fact that those people found themselves suddenly facing other people who were technologically more developed, richer, more powerful and whose ways of life had been proven more effective than theirs. This fact brings about different and opposite reactions, which are always negative: on one side an imitation, free of criticism, of everything the white man stands for; on the other side, especially in native intellectuals, a total rejection of Western civilization, including all it offers of what is good and of universal value. This is the "reverse racism" denounced by Senghor, among different groups of the new African elite.[2]

It is true that sooner or later any impact on the third world would have had to have been the impact of the West. The hypothesis of development in a vacuum is absurd. No people known to history has developed in isolation, free from foreign contacts. But if this impact had been made more gradually, with greater respect for local culture on the part of the West, and by way of evolution, not rupture, Africa and Asia would not now be experiencing the present cultural and psychological instability that is inevitably reflected in the political and social fields.

VARIOUS KINDS OF ECONOMIC EXPLOITATION

The theme of economic exploitation is vast and has been widely treated in many books about the third world. Colonial powers began with the principle that they must further their own interests and those of the mother country; therefore their operations in the economic sphere were often negative concerning the lands being colonized, most especially because their efforts were conditioned by foreign interests. Of these negative results, here are some examples:

—the imposition of a monoculture, producing exportable items, that enriched first of all the foreign company and neglected the production of food for the local people.

—the impoverishment of the soil because of irrational exploitation without any rotation of crops (planting for exportation was in the hands of foreigners who were not concerned about the future).

—obstacles to the development of native industries or simply, as in India, the suppression of already existing industries to make room for the invasion of English products, particularly textiles.

—the rise of parasite classes dependent on the colonial system's control of land and population—for example, country moneylenders who were a true plague in India; they were a part of the fiscal system introduced by the British, who assigned a certain class of people to collect taxes. The poorest country people who were not able to pay, especially in times of want, incurred lifelong debts and were bound to the moneylenders until death. Even today this system is one of the major obstacles to the development of Indian agriculture.

—the paralysis and parasitism of the third sector—made up of members of a privileged and unproductive class—that resulted in the organization and administration of a whole economy geared to the functioning of external interests; this led to unproportional development in the colonies' administration, commerce, and various services that served the upper classes. With a low-yielding agriculture (except what was needed for export) and a nonexistent industry, colonies that achieved independence found themselves weighed down by the unproportionately large third sector and by the natives themselves, who dreamed about the very rewarding positions in this sector as, for example, colonial employees, transportation officials, accountants, messengers, and state bureaucrats. The colonial powers created this class, the members of the third sector, instead of concerning themselves with the development of the primary sector (agriculture) and the establishment of the secondary sector (industry).

The result of colonization on the economic plane was the creation of lands economically dependent on rich countries, without any real desire for their own autonomous development and with no further ambition but to serve the colonial powers. They became the suppliers of raw materials. They provided open markets for industrial products and profitable opportunities for commercial companies. Sometimes (as in the case of Algiers and the French) they were able to offer cheap labor for the national industries. In this way the economic submission of the third sector to the developed world was brought about. Today this is a huge stumbling block to the progress of poor countries. We do not say, as do others, that this is the principal cause of the poverty of the third world, because in our opinion this poverty is intrinsic to the third world and is due to the fact that there has been no cultural and social evolution. But, certainly, this represents a heavy mortgage on the future of the former colonies.

POSITIVE ASPECTS OF COLONIZATION

It would be erroneous to conclude from what has been said so far that Western colonization has done nothing positive for the third world and that it has been, as some authors (usually of Marxist inspiration) have written, the principal cause of today's underdevelopment. First, it should be noted that not all underdeveloped countries have been colonies, and not all colonies are underdeveloped countries—the United States, Canada, and Australia were colonies for centuries, yet they are among the most technically developed lands. Secondly, many poor countries have never known colonization—these include, among others, Spain, Portugal, Greece, and southern Italy in Europe; and China, Tibet, Mongolia, Iran, Turkey, Afghanistan, Arabia, and Thailand in Asia. In Africa, Liberia has been politically independent for more than a century, and Ethiopia was a colony for only five years. And Latin America won her independence before the middle of the last century.

It cannot be stated, therefore, that colonization and underdevelopment are two inseparable phenomena that explain one another; it would be wrong to reconstruct history on an hypothesis that has not been realized. To illustrate, some say that if the West had not conquered Africa, that continent today would be more advanced and more integrated according to its own traditional culture. Such reasoning has no foundation in fact. After all, if Africa had not been colonized by Europeans, it would have been colonized by Arabs, for they had already begun to do so. Or it might have been colonized by Indians, and this might have been even worse. In the second place, before its colonization, Africa (or, for that matter, Asia and Latin America) could not all alone have developed technically in a short time. In the third chapter of this book we explained why this is so. Not in its culture or in its history is to be found the premise that would lead it to modern development. If the Europeans had not gone to Africa, the black continent would probably be today, when the moon is being explored, just as it was more than five hundred years ago. Moreover, the Africans would now have found it much more difficult to begin their advance towards modern times.

As a rule, history is not made according to hypotheses. Colonization has taken place, and sooner or later would inevitably have taken place, although it could have been done in a far more humane manner and with a finer concern for the interests and the culture of those being colonized. Yet, in addition to the negative aspects already examined, there are some positive aspects of colonization that we will now briefly summarize.

(a) *The formation of the present nations of the third world.* From the political point of view, colonization has had positive effects. It has created the nations of the third world as we know them today, shaping their boundaries, communicating a sense of patriotism, and preparing the guidelines for a modern state. So general a statement could be challenged, this we know. Yet in a few pages we shall try to give a fairly complete picture of centuries of history to explain why we are convinced that the political side of colonization should be considered a positive value, despite its many negative aspects: for instance, the arbitrary divisions of the colonial territories without regard to geographical and ethnic factors; the brutal suppression of independence movements; the fostering or rekindling of century-old hatreds between races, religions, and tribes (the politics of "divide and conquer" practiced by England in India and Africa); and the failure in some instances to give adequate training to the leaders of new nations (the immense Congo at the moment of its independence from Belgium had only about ten black graduate students).

In a good part of the third world, few countries before colonization had fairly definite boundaries or were united under one ruler. Most of the present boundaries of the former colonies in India, Africa, Indonesia, and Latin America were the result of colonial conquest and the union of separate countries by the colonial powers. Native nationalism is a reaction to colonization that gave to widely different and often hostile peoples a new sense of patriotism. To mention only one—India, before the arrival of the English, was not a real nation; she began to unify only after the Congress Party was founded in 1885 as a result of the unanimous reaction of different peoples to English domination.

Obviously, the English did not favor the formation of nationalistic political parties in India or in any other colony; however, their formation became inevitable with the unifying of the peoples, the rise of the first modern native elite, and the imposition of a common language (India has had, even to this day, hundreds of languages; the same is true of Africa). In short, the very ideas that colonialism exported to the third world were responsible for its downfall: nation, fatherland, democracy, liberty, centralized government, precise and established boundaries.

In Africa the beneficent action of colonization in the political field is even clearer than in India. Today's black African countries were created by colonial conquest. Prior to the arrival of the foreigners, no native elite was prepared to govern a modern state and there was no sense of patriotism among the various peoples. One of the greatest obstacles to the development of the African continent was "Balkanization," that is, the excessive fragmentation of states. Colonizers sought to overcome this difficulty by creating countries of substantial size and large federations of several countries (British East Africa, Congo, Ruanda-Burundi, the Central African Federation, etc.). After independence the federations fell apart or no longer acted together. In many African lands—Nigeria, Congo, Sudan, Cameroon, Chad, etc.—the separatist tendency was strong. The presence of the colonial power overshadowed old tribal or religious struggles, and created a sense of unity among the different peoples.

(b) *The social-cultural evolution of static civilizations.* History shows that it was colonization that put an end to the static condition of the third world. Of this we have spoken in the preceding chapter. To repeat, the brutal destruction of the old culture admittedly had negative aspects, but by the same token it brought the people of the third world into direct contact with vital and universal principles that enabled them to begin to move toward progress. Had these peoples of other cultures not had contacts with the dynamic civilization of the West, they would not have experienced the "revolution of the ideas," which is always the first impulse towards progress—the dignity of man, the equality of all men, the proper relationship between man and nature, and the idea of history as linear advance, not cyclic return.

Today there has been a resurgence of appreciation for the authentic values of ancient cultures. Quite rightly the people of the third world are becoming more and more conscious that their evolution should proceed in accordance with their own traditions so that they may maintain their own identity in the human community. This statement, however, should be qualified in two ways. The first observation to be made is that the colonizers themselves (and this includes Christian missionaries), though they may have contributed to the decadence of the local culture, have also been the first to study those cultures. They have tried to make them known and helped to preserve many ancient witnesses to the past. History itself shows these contrasting aspects: on one hand, the colonizers did not value and preserve local cultures; on the other, they studied them and brought about a renaissance. It is impossible today to write a history of African culture without referring to a largely European bibliography. This is also true of the history of Hinduism, Buddhism, Oriental cultures, ancient texts, archaeological discoveries, and restoration of monuments. The majority of these authors were colonizers or missionaries. From this point of view, therefore, colonization has had some undeniable beneficial results, since it introduced Western students to the culture of the third world and thus made possible the study and preservation of relics of the past.

The second observation to be made is this: Even now there is a tendency to idealize the precolonial society of the third world, presenting it as a kind of earthly paradise in which hunger and war were unknown, and solidarity and equal distribution of goods prevailed. According to some authors it was Western civilization that brought to it war, slavery, and every kind of excess. This picture of the precolonial world is untrue. Indeed, another of the merits of colonization is to be found in its struggle against many inhumane customs and basically unjust social structures (this, despite its introduction of other forms of injustice) and the progress that has been made with the gradual advance from inhuman to more human conditions.

In pre-Columbian Mexico the Aztecs and the Toltecs offered mass human sacrifices and one of the chief reasons for wars of conquest was to procure victims for these sacrifices. In Africa there was cannibalism and human sacrifice. In India the widow was burned on her husband's funeral pyre. Throughout the third world, the condition of women was vastly improved by colonization through the suppression of child marriages, polygamy, and the buying and selling of women. At the beginning, slavery was a powerful institution that was encouraged and supported by the colonial powers; but in the nineteenth century they worked to abolish slavery and today it is to be found only in lands that have never been colonized, such as Arabia, Afghanistan, and Yemen. The domination of the stronger races and tribes was weakened by colonization, thus enabling minority groups to develop themselves. Among these minorities were the pariahs of India, and the tribal peoples of India and many Asiatic countries such as Burma and Vietnam. The Sudan Negro in the south was much better off under the English than he is today under the Arabs of the north.

(c) *Of all the former colonies, the more developed ones are those that were most colonized.* A visit to the third world shows that where a colonial power was in control for several decades, people and structures are more advanced than in regions where there was little colonization.[3] In India, for example, the native principalities that the English respected are the least developed in the country. I visited the state of Andhra in southeast India. It includes one section that was colonized and another, Nizam, that remained outside English influence. In both sections the people belong to the same race and speak the same language, Telega. However, in the regions that had been colonized—Vijayavada, for one—amazing progress is immediately evident in the paved streets, higher education, artificial irrigation through many canals and dikes, and the beginning of industrialization. In Nizam the situation is totally different. Even after twenty years of independence, there are no streets, no irrigation in the fields, few schools, a less developed population, and no industries at all.

I noted the same conditions when I went to East Africa. The two most advanced countries, Kenya and Uganda, had been the most thoroughly colonized and for a longer time. Conversely, Ethiopia and Tanzania are more backward because of less colonization. The five years of Italian rule in Ethiopia marked a period of major development and even today the economy of the nation depends largely on infrastructures created by Italian labor. This is not meant to be an approbation of the fascist war of conquest or of all the massacres. It is no more than a statement of truth, admitted by the Ethiopians themselves, that the brief presence of the Italians furthered the progress of the country.

German pre-World War I colonization in Tanzania is remembered with gratitude. The present roads and railway go back to that time. Yet the English protectorate is condemned because there was little colonization. For about fifty years Tanzania was left alone and made much less progress than did Kenya and Uganda which, during those years, were being intensively colonized by the English. Again I beg not to be misunderstood. In no way do I approve of the injustice, the massacres, and the exploitation of the people of Kenya and Uganda by the English. I only want to say that in spite of much that was negative and objectionable, these two colonies made progress while Tanzania remained without roads, schools, or modern agriculture. Within the countries that I visited, I could see a sharp difference between each region: where there had been no colonization the people were backward.

The Baganda tribe of southern Uganda were for a long time under the English, who exploited the land but built schools, roads, modern agriculture, and small industries able to handle the products of field and farm. Today the Baganda are the leading tribe of the country. However, in northern Uganda, the Karamojon tribe was not colonized, and its territory was closed even to missionaries, with the result that its precolonial backwardness never changed.

The contrast between the territories of the Baganda and Karamojon is startling. In one section there are villages and modern cities, roads, irrigation canals, growing industries, dikes, planned agriculture, almost 100 percent schooling, and railroads. In the other, where the English never penetrated, there is no sign of modern agriculture, except what the government and the missionaries are beginning to introduce. The first schools have been built, but the parents have yet to be convinced that they should send their children to them. The Karamojon, accustomed as they have always been to living a nomadic, pastoral life, hesitate to settle in villages. Tribes fight one another with such terrible ferocity that sometimes government forces have to intervene to prevent the total destruction of minority groups. This year drought caused a great famine and many village people literally died of hunger. In a word, life in this section is still precolonial in spite of the praiseworthy efforts of the Uganda government during these last years.

What I saw in Kenya was much the same. The civilized Kikuyu, Luo and Meru who lived in the center of the country had been colonized. Still very backward are the Turkana, the Masai, and the Borana, who did not come under English influence.

I repeat, lest I be misunderstood, that colonization had many faults that cannot be considered lightly, and as Christians we must be ashamed that other Christians have done what they did. But a certain widely held anticolonial myth does not correspond to the facts. From the point of view of modern progress the European colonization of the third world had many positive results that cannot be ignored.

Of course colonization inspired by Christian principles could have done much more for the development of these colonies. The colonization of the third world was not the best possible. Yet in spite of all its faults and failures it can be said that the basic cause of underdevelopment was certainly not European colonization. The Europeans did not reduce a developed people to poverty, they did not create conditions of underdevelopment in countries already enjoying a high standard of living, as in the case of the Soviet colonization of Czechoslovakia. True, they did upset the balance of subsistence, thus creating new forms of imbalance and injustice; but in spite of this, the colonized people were set upon the path leading to modern progress.

THE SCANDAL OF INTERNATIONAL TRADE

The discussion of the negative and positive aspects of colonization is of value today inasmuch as it leads to a second more timely problem—economic, political, and cultural neocolonialism. Although military occupation and direct colonization have come to an end, underdeveloped countries are still under the dominion of European powers and the United States. This phenomenon is known as neocolonialism, which is a renewal of the old colonial domination under a new form.

Once again it must be said that this new form of Western domination has both positive and negative values for the development of the countries of the third world. It would be an oversimplification to condemn *a priori* and without distinction the relations of the developed world and the third world (this would mean the end of every kind of help and exchange) by claiming that between the rich and the poor the relation can only be domination and oppression on the one hand, submission on the other. Undoubtedly, as we have said, neocolonialism represents a great potential danger for poor countries, but at the same time it can be of help towards their development. Let us see why.

The principal accusation normally leveled against neocolonialism concerns the unjust commercial relations between rich and poor countries. This is a known fact and it has been denounced by Paul VI in Development of Peoples:

> Of course, highly industrialized nations export for the most part manufactured goods, while countries with less developed economies have only food, fibers, and other raw materials to sell. As a result of technical progress the value of manufactured goods is rapidly increasing and they can always find an adequate market. On the other hand, raw materials produced by underdeveloped countries are subject to wide and sudden fluctuations in price, a state of affairs far removed from the progressively increasing

value of industrial products. As a result, nations whose industrialization is limited are faced with serious difficulties when they have to rely on their exports to balance their economy and to carry out their plan for development. The poor nations become poorer while the rich ones become still richer (n. 57).

Here it would be superfluous to repeat the concrete details of the scandal of international trade. They may be found in every book in which world hunger is discussed. To take a specific case, Tanzania is the main source of an insecticidal powder derived from the dried flowers of the pyrethrum plant. There I learned that those farmers who had been persuaded to cultivate the pyrethrum because of its market value were all ruined in a few years. In 1962 a ton of pyrethrum was worth 225 pounds sterling. In 1969 the price of a ton had dropped to 80 pounds sterling. Why? Because European and American firms no longer made natural insecticide—for which pyrethrum was necessary—but they use instead chemical products that cost much less. Prices of almost all raw materials, with perhaps the exception of petroleum, continue to decline, while the cost of industrial products rises. For example, in 1954 the cost of an American jeep in Brazil was the equivalent of fourteen bags of coffee, in 1962 it was thirty-nine bags, in 1968 it was forty-five!

Hundreds of other examples could be cited. They are provided by the conferences in Geneva in 1964, in New Delhi in 1968, and in Santiago in 1972 organized by UNCTAD (United Nations Conference on Trade and Development) for the regulation of international trade. These three conferences, in which technicians and representatives from almost every country in the world participated, ended in a deadlock. All agreed that, alone, the law of supply and demand no longer operates, but they could find no solution to the problem that would be acceptable to all.

The problem is very complex. The rich countries are selfish in their demands, and some poor countries do not wish to regulate the production of raw materials. Here are some aspects of the question that are not always considered and that give some idea of the difficulty in reaching a conclusion:

(a) Poor countries tend to increase their production of raw materials, especially agricultural products. This means that the market is soon saturated, prices fall, and vast stockpiles of unsold products accumulate. Thirty or forty years ago when Brazil was the only country producing coffee, prices were high. Today almost forty countries produce coffee: Colombia, Mexico, Ecuador, Haiti, Kenya, Uganda, Tanzania, Ivory Coast, Burundi, and others. It would be absurd to think that all this coffee could be sold. A drop in price was inevitable. Furthermore, Brazil, for example, could sell only a little more than half of its production in 1965. The next year a most unusual frost destroyed millions of coffee plants in the state of Parana. I was in Brazil at the time and remember the banner headlines in the newspapers, rejoicing that it would not be necessary to destroy an important part of its coffee production for which there was no market.

What has been said about coffee could be repeated about other valuable agricultural products: bananas, cotton, cocoa, tea, etc.

In 1967, in preparation for the 1968 New Delhi Conference to which we have already alluded, the countries of the third world (eighty-eight in all) met in Algiers to discuss, among other topics, how to reduce the overproduction of materials for which surpluses already existed. This conference, like so many others, yielded meager results because no country wanted to reduce its production of valuable agricultural products. Each nation, from its own point of view, could have been right: Why, after having taken so much trouble to set up modern methods of planting coffee or tea, should these be destroyed to give another nation a better market? How could a country do this if the product in question was the only, or the principal, source of foreign capital in its national economy? All this seemed logical, but the result was that each nation produced too much, and sold its products at constantly lower prices.

(b) Rich countries tend to replace raw materials by synthetics produced in laboratories, which cost much less. We have spoken of the collapse of the price of pyrethrum, produced in Tanzania. In recent years, makers of insecticides discovered chemicals far cheaper and more effective than pyrethrum, which had to be sold at a price that scarcely covered production costs. The same might be said of cotton (synthetic threads were used instead); natural rubber (in many ways artificial rubber is superior for many products); oil products, such as palm oil; cocoa; peanuts; cane sugar (a substitute for the one extracted from beetroot). Many minerals are no longer needed—among these, carbon and magnesium.

We do not want to introduce a technical discussion here. The solution of the problem is a complex one to which all must contribute. This means restricting the production of certain raw materials, lowering the tariffs on third-world products, and delaying the use of new inventions until countries producing raw materials are able to readapt their crops and establish "integration funds" to compensate for any too sudden rise or fall in prices. Too little has been done up to the present time, apart from some particular agreements between some rich and poor countries, or between the Common Market and African countries (for example, Italy buys bananas from its former colony, Somalia, at a price two-thirds higher than that on the international market). Let us conclude with three affirmations:

It cannot be denied that some of the new poor countries have been unfairly treated in international trade. In the following two paragraphs of Development of Peoples Paul VI declares that the play of free exchange in international trade is good when the economic condition of the two contrasting parties is not too desperate:

> . . . the rule of free trade, taken by itself, is no longer able to govern international relations. Its advantages are certainly evident when the parties involved are not affected by any excessive inequalities of economic power: it is an incentive to progress and a reward for effort. That is why industrially developed countries see in it a law of justice. But the situation is no longer the same when economic conditions differ too widely from country to country: prices which are "freely" set in the market can produce unfair results. One must recognize that it is the fundamental principle of liberalism, as the rule of commercial exchange, which is questioned here (n. 58).

> The teaching of Leo XIII in *Rerum Novarum* [The Condition of Labor] is still valid: if the positions of the contracting parties are too unequal, the consent of the parties does not suffice to guarantee the justice of their contract, and the rule of free agreement remains subservient to the demands of the natural law. What was true of the just wage of the individual is also true of internatinal contracts: an economy of exchange can no longer be based solely ·on the law of free competition, a law which, in its turn, too often creates an economic dictatorship. Freedom of trade is fair only if it is subject to the demands of social justice (n. 59).

It should be remembered that in this complex question there is no miraculous solution. As the UN delegate from Argentina, Raúl Prebisch, said at the Algiers Conference to which we have already referred:

> We are cherishing a great illusion that will rebound on our countries if we think that the chaos of international trade can be set in order with a simple summit agreement. . . . What is needed is total reorganization of the price system, market control, various kinds of protectionism, production of raw materials, and their consumption. Progress can be made only step by step.

To sum it all up, the importance of the fair regulation of international trade in the development of the third world has been greatly overvalued. Some writers and lecturers seem to think that this is the fundamental condition for the advance of poor people. Perhaps they reach this conclusion because it is so easy to describe the elementary mechanism of the rise and fall of prices. Also, if international trade were regulated in a just manner, poor countries would have the benefit—certainly one not to be despised—of knowing in advance the selling price of their products, and thus avoid incurring grave losses. However, though they could better plan state balances, they would certainly not have much more money. The overproduction of raw materials should in every instance be reduced, and each country ought to agree to self-imposed limitations. There are millions of tons of coffee or cocoa that are of no use to anyone, so it is obvious that the producers ought to cut down on their production.

To conclude, let us fight for fairness in international trade, but let us not make a myth about it as if it were the key to the whole development of the third world.

NEGATIVE ASPECTS OF NEOCOLONIALISM

Another aspect of neocolonialism is the economic domination of rich countries over poor ones, not only on the commercial plane, as has been said, but with the control and exploitation of the very economy of poor countries. Here are some elements of this aspect:

(a) *Investment of private capital in the third world.* In 1968 private firms of rich Western lands invested a total of 5.8 million dollars in poor countries;[4] of this sum, 40 percent was in petroleum. It has been estimated that from 1955 to 1966 this kind of investment stood at 35 millions. When private foreign capital tends to dominate the inner sectors of the economy of a poor country, the latter is no longer free. The director of the political and financial section of OECD (Organization for Economic Cooperation and Development), Hellmut Fuehrer, wrote:

> Foreign investment is, in certain cases, on so large a scale that it dominates the economic and political life of a country. Some underdeveloped lands found that a single company or a group of investors controlled the whole country. This would never happen in an industrialized country where there was an abundance of local capital.[5]

It is not hard to find concrete examples of this economic domination: oil companies in the Midle East, banana and other tropical-fruit companies in Central America. Furthermore, though to a smaller extent in less evolved lands, most modern industry is in the hands of foreign capitalists and technicians. This is particularly true of Africa, where companies in former colonies continue to control modern sectors of the economy, both industrial and agricultural (with the exception of merely subsistence agriculture).

Another accusation that has been made about private investments in the third world is that the profit level is too high and consequently constitutes a real exploitation of the natural resources and the local labor. These yield an interest rate of from 10 to 12 percent per year, while in developed countries it is no more than 7 to 9 percent. The Argentine economist, Prebisch, at the 1964 Conference of Geneva on International Trade to which we have referred, revealed that the profits the rich countries make in poor countries are greater than the sum originally invested. He added that from 1950 to 1961 the investment of foreign capital in the minerals and agriculture of Latin America totalled nine million dollars, but the sum the investors brought back was thirteen million dollars. In this case, Prebisch justly pointed out, while it was the poor who had given money to the rich, the rich emerged as seemingly generous benefactors.

(b) *Government help, combined with political blackmail.* It is known that the governments of developed countries prefer to give their help directly to poor countries, rather than through the UN and its organizations, and to make bilateral agreements with each single poor country, one by one. Such government help is too self-serving. It is predicated on political motives, prestige, and competition, so that the whole question of aid is falsified. Not only are the governments of these poor countries unable to make their own long-term development programs (because they do not know whether the donor nations will continue in their present line of thinking), but they must also be subjected to the political and economic blackmail of those who help them. Cuba, prior to the Castro regime, was bound to the United States. It was practically an American political and economic colony. Today it has become a colony of Soviet Russia with whom it has contracted a colossal debt which forces it to maintain a specific political orientation. No matter what Castro wants, he cannot now free himself from Soviet control unless he stages another total revolution like that of 1959. Were he to do this, he would inevitably find himself once again under some other controlling power.

To a lesser extent all poor countries find themselves more or less dependent on one of the great powers. Consequently this dependence is economic and hence political. This prevents complete freedom of action because important decisions will be made thousands of miles away and will be determined solely by the interests of the major power. The impossibility of rebelling in such a situation (without passing from one dependency to another, as in the case of Cuba), depends on two factors. First of all, poor countries must base their economy on the exportation of raw materials (agricultural or mineral). Given the superabundance of the production of these raw materials, developed nations can blackmail poor nations by threatening to stop purchases; if they do stop buying, they are able in a few years to ruin their economy (for example, the United States is trying "to bring Castro back to reason" by not buying his sugar). The second factor involves the debts which poor countries incur towards the rich. These grow larger year by year for many reasons: economic crises, scanty returns from newly established industries, compounding of interest, etc. According to the Pearson Report these debts increased 14 percent in 1960,[6] and in June 1968 the public debt owed by poor countries to rich countries was about 475 billions of dollars. Often the new sums of money that some poor countries

received year by year were not large enough to pay old debts contracted in the past.

(c) *The economic control of poor countries is sometimes exercised directly
through the dominating presence of foreigners in newly independent countries.*
Throughout Africa the question of "Africanization" is bitterly de-
bated. This is an effort to persuade the different governments to
replace white men and Indians by black men in positions of authority
in industry, schools of higher education, and commerce. We shall
see later how difficult it is to answer this just request of the Africans.
The fact remains that in different parts of the third world—most
especially in Africa—foreigners (Indians, Syrians, Pakistani) still
hold key positions in almost every sector of modern life, with the
possible exception of strictly local affairs. For example, in various
countries a law designed to bring about Africanization requires that
a Negro must be at the head of certain industries. But once the
law is made, a way around it is soon found. The foreigners find
a figurehead to whom they pay a good stipend and allow him to
make no decisions.

POOR COUNTRIES NEED RICH COUNTRIES

The economic and political neocolonialism that we have briefly
described is gravely unjust and extremely harmful to the dignity
of countries that are, in theory, independent. The blame for political
and economic blackmail, for the horrible exploitation, lies with the
rich nations and the world's system of economic-political relations,
in which force always prevails and the stronger is always right.
A Christian attempt to face up to this iniquitous state of affairs
requires condemnation and radical change. To be effective, any
such condemnation should be rational, and not based simply on
wishful thinking. Very often in this area there is danger of irrational
thinking, of hypothetical solutions, that have not the slightest possibility of becoming effective.

Jean-Marie Domenach, the director of *Esprit*, a periodical that
is a long way from being conservative, has written a strongly polemical article attacking Claude Julien's book, *America's Empire*.[7] He dis-
proves the book's two basic affirmations that (1) American prosperity

depends on the exploitation of poor countries (America's entire foreign trade with poor and rich countries comprises no more than 4 percent of the gross national product), and (2) poor countries are poor because of the economic imperialism of America or, to put it more generally, of rich countries. According to Domenach, a condemnation of world economic imperialism should not obscure the vision of things as they really are.[8]

Let us face neocolonialism realistically. We have pointed out its errors. Now let us complete this description by stating its merits. Positive aspects are not lacking.

(a) Recent years have seen enormous hostility toward the idea of and financial assistance to poor countries. The Most Reverend Antonios Fragoso, Bishop of Cratens, Brazil, has long held this view:

> Help towards development is offered by rich countries. Yet in my experience it seems that international help is an important obstacle to our development in Latin America. This help hinders our development and increases our alienation. We do not need technicians from rich countries . . . we do not need money from rich countries, because this money corrupts us a little more. As a result we grow accustomed to seeking solutions for our problems from others. We must have courage to see clearly and to ask that this help cease.[9]

Every opinion deserves respect but views such as these are unreasonable; they were probably employed for rhetorical effect during a conference, and need not be taken literally. There is a real abyss in the area of economic development between rich and poor countries. This can be seen in the standard of living and modern production but this does not mean that help, loans, investments, and foreign technicians need be excluded. Justice undoubtedly demands that the whole system of international help to the underdeveloped world be improved. But that the help of rich nations to poor nations should be totally abolished is absurd.

It is true that rich countries receive economic advantages from the investments that they make in poor countries, but they also help the government and local population through wages and taxes, the construction of roads and ports, the training of workers and native technicians, and the support of local industries. Of course the governments of poor countries ought to exercise a majority control over their investments so that the exportation of valuable products would be regulated to insure a favorable combination of mixed (foreign and local) capital, to impose a fair tax on profits, and to require short-term contracts that contain clauses allowing for revision after a few years. But to believe that underdeveloped lands could, by themselves, bring about their own development is one of the "unreasonable" statements denounced by Domenach.

Let us examine some specific illustrations of this truth. About twenty years ago in Brazil immense fields of petroleum were found in Amazonia. An American company asked the Brazilian government for permission to open up this find. Getulio Vargas, who was then the dictator, was in a difficult political position, and thought he could use this occasion to stimulate feelings of nationalism. He therefore refused the American firm's request and publicized the slogan: "The petroleum is ours!" words that are still famous in Brazil. A state company, Petrobras, was established to produce Brazilian petroleum. That was in 1953. From that year to this no petroleum has yet been extracted. Consequently, Brazil, one of the richest countries in the world, must import American petroleum from Venezuela.

Some might say that at least Brazil has prevented foreigners from exploiting its petroleum. The question, however, is whether Brazil, when able by itself to extract the petroleum, will find the undertaking necessary or profitable. Sources of power have already changed many times in recent decades. Wood has been replaced by coal, and electricity by atomic energy, solar energy, and energy produced by high and low tides (on ocean shores where the difference is measured in yards, there is a great source of power that spontaneously repeats itself twice a day).

It would be sad if Brazil, who is now paying dearly for its nationalist intransigence in refusing to allow others to extract its petroleum, should find itself twenty years from now—when it is finally able to extract the oil—floating in a sea of petroleum that no one wants because other nations will then be using solar or tidal or atomic energy. It would not be the first time that something like this has happened. For instance, if Brazil decided today to allow rich countries to develop the coal that is so close to the surface of the soil in Amazonia, I doubt that there would be much demand for a mineral that has been largely superseded. This, then, is what has happened to a natural resource that was worth something twenty years ago and today is of no use to anyone. Perhaps that same thing will happen tomorrow to the country's petroleum.

To take another example from Brazil, one of the few mineral concessions that the Brazilian government granted in Amazonia was that of mining manganese in the Amapà territory. This enormous deposit, too, is near the surface of the earth. For fifteen years an American firm, ICOMG, has literally removed some hills that are almost pure manganese. To extract this mineral the company has built—where before there was nothing—two towns, a railroad less than 100 miles long (the only one in Amazonia), a modern port, and elementary and professional schools for the people (it was impossible to import all the workers from America). The taxes that ICOMG pays to the government of the Amapà territory represent the major source of income in that depressed area. With this money the great dike of Paredâo and other public works were built. In Amapà ICOMG, together with the Italian missionaries of PIME and some Japanese groups, is the most important element of progress in the territory. Today the mining of manganese is almost wholly in the hands of Brazilians. It is not important that the company continues to make huge profits because of the benefits that it has created for the local population. I do not think a case like this can be called "exploitation," since if it were not for the American firm, the manganese would still be buried in the forests and Amapà would be even more backward. Moreover, manganese will probably decrease in importance in the future.

(b) Another aspect of neocolonialism that has polarized the countries of the third world is the presence of foreigners in key positions. This may be seen in Africa, where governments are doing all that is possible to "Africanize" their economy, administration, and other modern sectors of national life. Where local talent has not yet been prepared, foreign technicians must be allowed to continue their work on an essential activity or it will have to stop.

In Kenya I was able to secure direct information about Africanization. I found some instances in which it was a success, some in which it was a failure. In primary and secondary education, the liberal arts, politics and journalism, Africans have fairly easily replaced foreigners. But in other fields the results have been different.

In 1966 a law was passed, handing over the technical direction of the country's one and only port, Mombasa, to the Africans; the English technicians were dismissed. In three months, traffic at the port was practically paralyzed, and the government had to hire other Europeans. The same thing happened to the management of the railroad that today is under the direction of white technicians. In commerce, also, something similar occurred, when the Indians were expelled, and others then gradually withdrew in fear. A crisis of distribution arose, and in response to popular demand the government had to revoke the degree of expulsion of those Indians who were not Kenya citizens.

The most difficult case was that of workers who supported the "freedom fighters" (Mau Mau). They had fought against the English to win back their highland territory, which had been taken from them at the beginning of the century. After independence much arable land was taken from the English and given to the Mau Mau, who formed cooperatives for its cultivation. The number of English workers was reduced from five thousand to fifteen hundred. This movement of expropriation now has ceased and a movement in the opposite direction has begun. The Europeans who remained are buying land from the Mau Mau. I understand that the lands remaining in the hands of the English have continued to prosper, while those that passed to the Mau Mau are bankrupt. Many have been abandoned; others produce only enough for the owners to support their families. In a situation like this, what should the government of Kenya do? Dispatch the remaining English? Or allow them to continue to occupy uncultivated land? The latter course would give work to the natives, and increase both agricultural production and tax payments to the government. Near Nairobi I did see modern farms directed by African graduates of agricultural high schools. These, however, are still very few in number and are not yet able to replace the whole white colony.[10]

In one of the last things he wrote before his assassination, Tom Mboya, Economic Planning Minister, and the founder of syndicalism in Kenya, replied to a charge made by a member of the opposition that the Kenya government had been very slow in bringing about the "Africanization of the sectors." Here are some of Mboya's remarks:

In Kenya it is not so much a question of the fair distribution of the results of progress already accomplished, but rather to do everything possible to multiply these results. . . . The solution to all these problems is rapid economic growth. . . . If Africanization is achieved at the cost of this growth, we will have reached a decadent standard of living. Therefore in Kenya priority should be given to planning for growth. . . . In our country and in many other countries on the way to development, the most important preoccupation is not the nationalization of already existing industries but rather the creation of new industries.[11]

Kenya is the classic example of a land controlled by foreigners. Certainly it is one of the least Africanized of all Africa. The presence of 43,000 Europeans and 200,000 Indians (from Goa or from Pakistan), all holding high positions in the economy or technology, supports this affirmation and explains why the opposition to "slow Africanization" of the government is so strong among the intellectual classes. It is as though, in a white nation, 200,000 Negroes, Chinese, and Indians out of a population of one million held all the executive offices, rights of ownership, and the most lucrative economic positions. The leader of the opposition, Oginga Odinga, denounced this situation in a violently polemical book with the significant title: *Not Yet Uhuru* [*Independent*]?[12] These words became a slogan constantly repeated in newspapers and magazines. Jomo Kenyatta replied with a book of his own, *Suffering Without Bitterness*,[13] in which he claimed that too rapid an advance would bring the country to economic chaos and that executive offices should be won by experience and competence, not by the color of the skin. Only a leader like Kenyatta with a prestigious popular following could make such a statement with impunity in the Africa of today.

Neocolonialism in Kenya has had for the most part positive results. The socioeconomic picture that Kenya presents is one of the best in Africa. The population increase averages 2.7 percent, while the growth of the gross national product was 14.4 percent in 1966 and 13.5 percent in 1967—an average that is extremely rare in Africa. Secondary schools have tripled in the last five years, and elementary education is practically universal among the larger and more evolved tribes. In sanitary facilities, professional training, small industries, transportation, and other essential areas, Kenya is making great progress in comparison to the majority of other African countries. Ample proof of this can be seen when one visits not only its cities but also its rural sections, and then visits seven or eight other African countries. It is true that revenues in Kenya are unevenly distributed. It is true, too, that foreigners control the economy. But as the country grows, native technicians and an idigenous executive class are being trained, and local capital is being developed so that the country can enjoy greater freedom tomorrow.

THE REAL DANGER OF NEOCOLONIALISM
IS TO BE FOUND IN THE CULTURAL ORDER

To conclude, relations between rich and poor countries in this post-colonial and neocolonial period are not, as is commonly believed, as simple as the facile Marxist theory makes them out to be, when it describes international society as composed of the exploiters and the exploited, with the third world (the exploited) on one side, and the imperialists and neocolonials (the exploiters) on the other. To this simplistic but subjective manner of viewing the world situation corresponds the principle theory of "armed revolution, no matter what the cost." This is perfectly logical if we accept the categories of exploiters and exploited. The countries of the third world, according to this theory, should suddenly and totally rebel against Western neocolonialism; nationalize foreign companies; expel all foreigners; and, if necessary, break off all relations with former colonial and imperialist powers. In other words, the best way to develop would be to have a revolution like that of China or Cuba.

At this point we do not want to dispute this position. This is for the people of the third world to decide. We cannot make the decision for them. Here we must try to understand the mechanism of underdevelopment and development so that, knowing their causes, we can make our contribution towards an equitable solution.

We hold that the underdevelopment of the third world is ultimately caused not by oppression coming from without, but because certain peoples—through no fault of their own—did not possess the germs of development and therefore were unable to organize themselves before their contact with the West; consequently they made no thrust toward the future, no movement toward progress. The violent clash with the West awakened these peoples, confronted them with new ideas, new methods, and new insights into development. This was the beginning of the advance, yet it is necessarily slow because most of them still do not understand the new ideas about man's dignity, equality, and progress, and their rights and duties as members of a modern society.

In this vision the West has failed to take a positive stand. As we have said before, the failures of colonialism are manifold; the faults of neocolonialism, very serious. To the third world the West was and is ambivalent—in some ways negative, in other ways positive.

Father L. J. Lebret has written that when a people are in "a static period," their culture and work extend only as far as is necessary to provide a means of survival; that is why they do not advance but remain just as they always have been.[14] But when they encounter a culture that is scientific, technical, or commercial, their traditional collective life is shaken in its very depths. Their advance towards progress begins at the moment of meeting with a dynamic civilization that transmits the principles and methods of progress. The clash therefore is beneficial, yet not without pain and destruction.

But Father Lebret insists that the development of a people (just like that of an individual man) should not be based on models imported from without. Every people ought to be free to make their own decisions and to develop their own culture according to the spirit of their own history and personality. From beyond their borders they should borrow principles that are universally valid (the dignity of man, for one) and scientific methods of production and of controlling nature, through the introduction of machinery, the construction of roads, etc. But the organization of society, the spirit of development, should be their own.

In other words the greatest danger of neocolonialism is not on the economic level as the Marxist thesis claims. On the economic and technical level, poor countries need rich countries. These commercial, industrial, financial, and technical relations should be just, and they should be controlled by the international community so that the dignity of small countries is not jeopardized. Such relations are necessary, and it would be absurd to cut them off violently in order to preserve an absolute freedom of action that no country enjoys today, least of all small and poor lands. Cuba is a case in point. It escaped from American domination to Soviet domination and is paying a very heavy price. The same reasoning applies to a certain extent to countries that are developed. For example, how free is Italy in the field of international politics? In its commercial relations with communist countries? In industrial production leading to a higher level? The world is constantly advancing towards interdependence in every sector. The touchy nationalism of some third world lands is old-fashioned.

The real danger of neocolonialism is its effect on the cultural order. This is little understood. It is easier and more provocative to describe commercial and economic exploitation than to speak in terms of culture.

Kenya's minister of education, J. G. Kiano, recently denounced this attitude. He wrote:

> At the moment of independence in 1963, Kenya inherited an educational system modeled almost exclusively on the English pattern. Its aim was to form a class of blacks that was foreign in its thinking, culture, and conduct.[15]

The drama of the third world does not primarily involve the escape from the economic domination of rich countries (although this is an important problem, it cannot be denied that, while furthering their own interests, wealthy nations can still bring benefits to poor countries). Rather, it is to avoid cultural colonialism through the imposition of forms of development, either capitalist or Marxist, originating in other continents and therefore alien to peoples of different cultures. A country's material progress cannot be paid for by the loss of its soul or the loss of the traditional culture that represents its identity.

Today we are witnessing a massive effort at "plagiarism" on the part of both capitalist and communist powers. (To some extent Christian churches are guilty of the same thing when they attempt to impose on the universally valid principles of Christ's message ecclesial structures that belong to the West.) Neocolonial culture is particularly prominent in the political field with its attempts to draw the third-world countries into its own particular party in order to establish a capitalist or Marxist pattern of society. It also insinuates itself into other sectors of civil life, profoundly influencing the teaching, the cultural industry, mentality, the moral sense, the art, folklore, etc., of the people.

The painful tension of the third world arises from the *difficult balance* that has to be achieved between the necessity of technical and material progress (because of the indispensable contacts with, and dependence on, the developed world) and the preservation of traditional values. Underdeveloped countries want to develop yet remain themselves. Today this is especially difficult because their own evolution is taking place during a period of intensive cultural change. There is no time for them to adapt themselves as they should to the needs of the modern world, driven as they are by the urgency to improve their economy and standard of living, and consequently to bring about rapid changes in their traditional structures. The slow development that lasted for centuries in Europe must be completed within a few decades in Asia and Africa.

The disappearance of an old culture, besides being a loss for all mankind, will always be more deeply felt in the third world. Little by little these people will free themselves from the slavery into which need has driven them, and gradually become aware of the authentic and irreparable loss that the West has inflicted on them by forcing them into a soulless model of development. In the future, the struggle between the capitalist and Marxist West will take place more and more on the political-cultural level than on the economic level. It will be a confrontation and contrast of civilizations, not of economic systems. Economies integrate more easily than cultures.

In a most interesting volume, the Indian historian Correia-Alfonso has described the frustrations of the modern Indian in contact with the West. India, he says, in the process of being Westernized, is becoming materialistic-minded and facing the loss of its soul.[16] The cry of alarm sounded earlier by Gandhi as well as the philosopher and president of India, Sarvepalli Radhakrishnan, is still valid today in all other countries possessing an ancient spiritual civilization.

Writing of the injury to the third world caused by colonialism and neocolonialism in their imposition of a model of materialistic life, Christopher Dawson has said:

> The new scientific culture lacks any kind of spiritual background. It is an immense complex of methods and specializations without any guiding spirit, without any basis of common values, without any spiritual aim that would provide some kind of unity. This was not evident as long as modern science was restricted to

the people of the West and was linked with communistic and liberal ideology. Now that modern science has spread all over the world, its neutral character and its spiritual vacuum has been revealed. We are living in a world of laicized scientific culture that is a body without a soul, while on the other hand religion stands apart, a spirit without a body.[17]

And Correia-Alfonso says further:

The whole world offers the spectacle of an acute spiritual conflict, a kind of social schizophrenia that separates the spirit of a society from an amoral will to power, served by human skill, religious faith and moral idealism powerless to influence human life.[18]

This is the central point of the relations between the developed and the underdeveloped world that we must keep in mind to bring our subject to its conclusion in the pages that follow.

FOOTNOTES

1. Cf. G. Guariglia, "I movimenti profetico-salvifici e le missioni" in *Le Missioni Cattoliche*, Milan, August/September, 1960, pp. 258, 269; and V. Lanternari, "movimenti religiosi di libertà e di slavezza dei popoli oppressi," Feltrinelli, Milan, 1960.

2. A classic example of "reverse racism" is found in the volume of Frantz Fanon, *The Wretched of the Earth*. The author reveals such a profound and total hatred of the whites, without any exceptions, as to horrify the reader.

3. The Swedish scholar Gunnar Myrdal, a specialist in the economic problems of the third world and not known for any tenderness in dealing with colonialism, writes in his classic, *Economic Theory and Under-developed Regions* (Very 1958 p. 62): "It is said that the economic activity of the colonizers furthered their own economic expansion and that without this particular form of colonial activity their own economic development would not have taken place. . . . In many instances the colonies developed more than they would have had they remained independent."

4. L. B. Pearson, *Vers une action commune pour le développement du tiers monde*, Denöel, Paris, 1969, p. 140.

5. "The Role of Private Foreign Investment in Economic Development," in *The OECD Observer*, September 1966, p. 43.

6. Pearson, *op. cit.*, p. 109.

7. New York: Pantheon, 1971.

8. "L'empire américain," in *Esprit*, April 1969, p. 642.

9. *La Croix*, Paris, December 7, 1968, p. 14.

10. For this whole problem, consult: R. Gavin, "Eimination du déséquilibre racial dans l'emploi au Kenya," in *Revue Internationale du Travail*, Geneva, January/February 1967, pp. 70-88.

11. "Sessional paper n. 10: It Is African and It Is Socialism," *East African journal*, Nairobi, May 1969, pp. 15-22.

12. Hainemann, Nairobi, 1967.

13. East African Publishing House, Nairobi, 1968.

14. *Progresso e solidarietà fra i popoli*, Borla, Turin, 1967, pp. 83-101.

15. "Africans, Not Carbon Copies of Foreign Societies," *The Kenya Teacher*, Nairobi, 1968, no. 5, pp. 5-9.

16. *L'anima dell' India moderna*, P.I.M.E., Milan, 1963.

17. *Religion and Culture*, pp. 214-216.

18. *Op. cit.*, p. 39.

HOW TO INVOLVE
ONE'S SELF IN
HELPING
THE THIRD WORLD

5

We asked in the preceding chapters why the third world is economically and technically underdeveloped in relation to the West, and we documented our answer that the radical cause of this underdevelopment is essentially internal to the third world itself. This means that the failure to develop is due to the lack of an inner drive to progress, aggravated by the violent impact of colonization with a static culture which has destroyed the balance between subsistence and cultural psychology. There are today many other obstacles to this forward march of countries and continents, such as commercial, political, and cultural neocolonialism.

A HUMAN DRAMA INVOLVING ALL

Now we ask: What are our responsibilities towards the third world? What ought we, as Christians in a developed world, do for those who have not yet begun to advance or for those who are progressing very slowly?

Here we cannot argue about the concrete measures that governments and international organizations ought to take to favor the development of the third world. It would be necessary to write at least another book to examine the financial, commercial, political, and cultural aspects of the whole complex problem. To give an example: Consider the highly complicated question of the regulation of trade in raw materials and in commercial exchange between rich and poor countries. After three international conferences in Geneva, Algiers, and New Delhi, in which dozens of states and many experts participated, we are still working on the methods to be used for implementing the few decisions already taken—that is, those that could be explained. But no one had been able to set forth in detail the steps that should be taken to regulate international trade so that all concerned would be dealt with fairly. We are only in the initial phase of denouncing an injustice for which no one has yet found, even in theory, an adequate solution. Were we to discuss this question, still another book would have to be written.

In general we are able to say that the solution to underdevelopment is to be found in the elimination of all the internal and external obstacles to progress, to which we alluded in earlier chapters, that impede the forward advance of poor peoples. If it is a question of the commercial exploitation of rich countries in relation to poor countries, clearly this exploitation must cease. If the politics of the great powers prevent economically weak countries from any autonomous decision-making, clearly this form of power politics is to be condemned and changed into a politics of service. (Abbé Pierre has written: "The Christian who has more can use this 'more' to help those who have less.")

It is necessary, however, to conclude this book with a summary and a precise statement of our responsibility as individuals and as a people who are both Christian and rich. Otherwise the reader might conclude: "If these are the causes of underdevelopment, I am not involved. Let those who are concerned do something about it." Actually, the wretchedness and hunger of two-thirds of mankind is a colossal, explosive fact that involves everyone. If I live in a valley and a dam in the mountain collapses, releasing masses of water that rush down, destroying everything, I cannot excuse myself by saying that it was all the fault of those who built the dam. Apart from every other consideration of human solidarity and Christian charity, I am caught in the oncoming flood, whether willingly or unwillingly, and I ought to do something for the common welfare, my own as well as that of everyone else.

In the same way, the dramatic and explosive situation, in which two-thirds of all men find themselves, does in fact involve everyone:

individuals, states, churches, political parties, and trade unions—no one can escape from the responsibility of doing as much as possible to help the development of the countries of the third world. In 1960, when B. R. Sen, the director of FAO, opened the campaign against hunger, he said: "The first thing to be done is to create a sense of the urgency of the problem among all men and a special climate that will lead to concrete action."

A few months later, at a conference of the FAO on May 3, 1960, Pope John went even further: "No one today, in a world where distances no longer count, can excuse himself by saying that he does not know the needs of his brother and that the help his brother needs does not concern him. We are all jointly responsible for the underfed peoples."

FULL DEVELOPMENT IS POSSIBLE EVEN FOR THE THIRD WORLD

What, then, is to be done? How can we practically, and without any wishful thinking, fulfill our obligation to the third world as men and as Christians?

The first obligation seems to me to be the overcoming of pessimism and defeat in regard to the third world's development. Development is possible for all. Hunger can be overcome—at least we can try to do something about it. To think that God has not given man—that is, mankind—sufficient resources for the development of all is absurd.

There are far too many writers and experts, strongly active pessimists, who insist that the third world will never reach the levels attained by the West for the reasons that they lack the right kind of resources, their overpopulation impedes all progress, rich people take advantage of them and prevent their development, or other similar reasons. There are others, racists, who think that underdeveloped peoples are inferior to Westerners in intelligence, will power, and competence, and since they can never do what we have done, they are condemned to be the poor of the world.

We say that pessimism concerning this question not only runs counter to the hopes of these people and therefore is inhuman, not only has negative results inasmuch as it discourages any kind of zeal, but is clearly opposed to both logic and reality.

Pessimism is contrary to logic. If we believe in the fundamental equality of men, if we are not racists, we ought to admit that all people are equally capable of development. The fact that some are more backward than others in moving toward modern progress does not mean that they cannot, whenever conditions are suitable, take their place among the more advanced. It is merely a question of creating these "suitable conditions" for the development of a people.

Pessimism is contrary to the facts. In the last twenty to twenty-five years reality has given the lie to all pessimistic predictions. In 1950 William Vogt predicted that within one generation the resources of the earth would not suffice for all men. Today we know that this has been proven false. In the years immediately after the war, when the Japanese seemed in desperate straits, many learned Americans anticipated that this impoverished country, with so little land, could not support more than seventy to seventy-five million inhabitants. That is why the American occupying forces launched a vast birth control campaign there. Twenty years later all the most pessimistic predictions are seen to be wrong. Japan is now the third economic power in the world. It has more than a hundred million inhabitants, yet there are not enough workers available to keep pace with the economic development.[1] In 1969 the Japanese government issued a White Paper, reporting the decline in the birth rate and asking the people to have more children if they wished to maintain their present rhythm of development and reach an even higher standard of living.

Only 13 percent of Japan's land is arable. In 1957 Professor Harrison Brown of the Institute of Technology in California declared that the Japanese people had reached the maximum possible production of rice and foodstuffs. Nevertheless in 1969—with, to repeat, more than a hundred million inhabitants—there was an overproduction of rice and other farm products, and the government had to take steps to decrease rice production. Technicians currently in the Japanese Ministry of Agriculture foresee that if they do not cut back on the continuing and rapid increase of agricultural products, the Japanese within a few years will have far too much rice, prices will fall (even now they are government-supported), and there will be an agricultural collapse.

Similarly, only a few years ago—in 1965—René Dumont foresaw an inevitable food catastrophe in store for India, the failure of every agricultural plan, and general famine within a short time.[2] Today the agricultural situation in India has so improved with the introduction of more productive seed, artificial irrigation, and fertilizer that experts expect that the country will be self-supporting, as far as food is concerned, in a few years. Cereal production in 1969 was 22 percent higher than in 1965, the year of the food crisis that forced the government to give priority to the modernization of agriculture.

In the beginning of the 1960's many writers and experts of the pessimistic school warned of a general economic reversal. Besides Dumont, cited above, there were the Paddock brothers, Americans, who collaborated on a book discussing what they claimed would be a general famine in 1975. Now in the early seventies we hear similar forecasts that are supposed to be realized within a few years and that seem equally absurd. It is true that food production is not socioeconomic development. It is merely one of its basic conditions. But it is already a fact that all the ominous predictions of the past have proven untrue. The "green revolution," whose initiator, the American N. E. Borlany, received the Nobel Peace Prize in 1970, makes it possible to face with serenity the problem of mankind's future food supplies.[3] This is a first step towards the rational exploitation of the earth's resources and let us keep in mind as well the immense food potential of the oceans.

At the close of 1969 the Pearson Report was published. This was greeted by authorities as the most accurate and up-to-date investigation of progress among poor countries made in the last twenty years. The inquiry was conducted by eight experts and twenty-five investigators of many lands led by another Nobel Peace Prize winner, Lester B. Pearson, the former prime minister of Canada. This report is decidedly optimistic about the future of the third world and condemns the pessimistic forecasts and unjustifiable alarmism that have circled the globe in recent years, declaring them to be the fruit of scientifically unprovable hypotheses.[4]

The report shows in more than five hundred fact-filled pages that underdeveloped countries advanced much more rapidly today than underdeveloped European nations did in the last century. Consequently there are good reasons to hope that in the course of the next thirty-four years the poor countries of today can maintain their present trend so that they can offer their people conditions for a life worthy of man. Naturally, much remains to be done. The Pearson

Report is no ingenuous exultation over progress already achieved, but an earnest reminder to rich countries as well as poor, and to the international organizations of the UN, that they must continue pressing for more decisive implementation of present programs and better use of the means available. According to this report, based on the way things have been proceeding in the last twenty years, the joint development of all mankind is perfectly possible, and no country need be condemned to remain forever poor and in a position of inferiority among other countries.

The first condition for our support of the third world seems to be this: to avoid excessive optimism as well as excessive pessimism. Development is possible for all only if there is a serious will to joint development among all men and all countries.

THE AVOIDANCE OF THE ERRORS OF COLONIALISM

The second premise we wish to make is this: The development of a people is not a gift that comes ready-made from outside, but a suffering accepted by those directly concerned. In other words, all peoples, like all individual men, are first and foremost responsible for, and the makers of, their own development. But no people and no man can develop alone, in isolation, but ought to advance along the lines of reciprocal solidarity and mutual aid.

This is what Development of Peoples says:

> World unity, ever more effective, should allow all peoples to become the artisans of their destiny (n. 65). The peoples themselves . . . have the prime responsibility to work for their own development. But they will not bring this about in isolation (n. 77). There can be no progress toward the complete development of man without the simultaneous development of all humanity in the spirit of solidarity (n. 43).

Our intervention on behalf of third-world countries ought therefore to respect these two basic elements that may seem contradictory: (1) to intervene with generosity, justice, and competence, in order to help those on the way to development with all the necessary means (financial help, technical assistance, etc.); and (2) to intervene, not for the purpose of determining the path they should take toward development, but only to help them to see their way and to give them the means that will make it possible for them to become the protagonists of their own development.

In short, the rich peoples have the duty to offer a service, a disinterested collaboration. They should not attempt selfishly to further their own cause, that is, the politics that figured in their own development. Such fundamental choices are to be left to the free option of those to be helped. In Development of Peoples we read: "As sovereign states they have the right to conduct their own affairs, to decide on their policies, and to move freely towards the kind of society they choose (n. 54)."

The Pope adds that this laissez-faire policy in respect to the freedom of these peoples may be difficult at times:

> The task might seem impossible in those regions where the cares of day-to-day survival fill the entire existence of families so that they are incapable of planning the kind of work which would open the way to a future that is less desperate. These, however, are the men and women who must be helped, who must be persuaded to work for their own betterment and endeavor to acquire gradually the means to that end (n. 55).

The words of the Pope are echoed in the words of the leaders of the third world. Many times they have asked that their freedom to make decisions be respected. It is useless to say that the large and small nations are in total disagreement about the political aspects of "help," for under the guise of development, help and technical assistance are often accompanied by attempts to influence the basic choices of the people. Some of these attempts involve the previously mentioned political and economic blackmail, as well as military intervention or sales of arms to one side.

On the same plane of the great powers, however, let us place those individuals who, well intentioned though they may be, wish on their own to make political decisions affecting the South Americans or Africans. How often do we find men who—instead of helping these people in a concrete way to become aware of their dignity and their rights so that they might develop according to their own freely made decisions—waste much of their time arguing whether there is a need to use violence or to foment revolution. Instead of artlessly offering for the problems of Latin America (or for those

r continent) solutions that were effective elsewhere in
...., they should realize that they are committing, with the
...eans and on the level possible to them, the same errors that they
condemn in the great powers who pretend to be disinterested, but
whose own political and social choices are, in reality, imposed on
the underdeveloped peoples. This, instead of humbly putting themselves at the service of these people, whom they are supposed to
be guiding according to local politics.

Helder Camara, perhaps the greatest living prophet of the third
world, was asked how the youth organizations of the West could
help the third world. First he recalled the awakening of public opinion
in the West and the pressure that should be brought to bear on
their governments. Then he continued:

> In the second place, these organizations ought to support the
> third world by doing something practical, by concrete help. It
> would be absurd to sit with folded arms while waiting for govern-
> ments to act. Much can be done while waiting for government
> action. Above all, I would like to warn these organizations to
> guard against suggesting solutions that they have found for their
> own problems. We do not want to be treated as if we were
> mentally underdeveloped and believed to be incapable of dis-
> covering solutions for ourselves. To do this would be to practice
> *a form of cultural neocolonialism*. Give us concrete guidance and
> help. It is up to us to discover the solutions to our own problems.[5]

THREE ATTITUDES TO BE CONDEMNED

In the presence of the wretchedness of the third world, three attitudes
are often found. They are neither just nor helpful.

1. The attitude that has been labelled *cartierista*. This word has
been coined from the name of a French journalist, Raymond Cartier,
who said: "If the third world is hungry, it is no business of mine.
This is a fact for which I do not feel responsible, and therefore
it does not interest me. The French government and other governments of rich countries already have too many problems about their
own development. Payment made to poor countries is money wasted
because they do not know how to use it. They squander it in forms
of prestige and armaments. Therefore we should give them no gifts.

Poor countries are free and independent, let them look after themselves."

A similar position, which we will here summarize, is as antihuman, anti-Christian, antihistorical as can be imagined. This would encourage the people and governments of rich countries to lock themselves up within a selfish isolation, which, other considerations aside, would cost them dearly someday. In an address to the FAO as early as November 10, 1955, Pius XII issued this warning:

> Peoples favored by nature and cultural progress run the risk of a day of rude awakening if they do not take care in good time to assure to the less fortunate the means of living humanly and with dignity, and to begin to help them to develop.

2. A second attitude is found among those who are quick to make an offering, even a generous one; but they never go any further. This is the classic *mentality of almsgiving*, or "*beggar's mentality*." These people believe that in putting their hands in their pockets they have done their duty once and for all, and they take no interest in the day-to-day living of the third world. This is a widespread attitude; we might say that it is the most common of all, though it does mark an advance over the preceding position and over the ignorance of the problem that prevailed ten or fifteen years ago. The Campaign Against Hunger introduced by FAO in 1960 at least made known the gravity of mankind's situation, in which two out of every three men live in subhuman conditions, and aroused at least the sense of almsgiving. This may be a first step, but surely it is not enough.

3. A third attitude, just as ineffective as the second but for opposite reasons, is found among groups rather than among individuals. These groups base all their activities on behalf of the third world on a *hopeless denunciation of injustice*. This is an attack on capitalism and imperialism, on the failure of governments to take action, on the racist policy of South Africa, on the unfairness of international trade, and so forth. They argue, make protests, and attempt by various kinds of provocation to arouse public opinion and incite other actions of like nature.

All this seems to be one way, among many others, of forming an "easy conscience." The more one protests, the more one thinks he is at peace with himself and with his neighbor: he feels "involved," "uncomfortable," always ready to raise a protest against the injustices of the world. And it does not matter if the protest action is effective or not in freeing the third world; it does not matter whether it is or is not the best thing one can do to help the third world's people. Such an in-depth examination of reality does not seem of great importance. To denounce the injustices unquestionably is a duty, but concrete help to the third world is more important for its liberation than mere protests. It seems—at least, that is the impression one gets from personal contact with certain "protest groups" —that these young people, even with all their generosity and good-will, are not serving the third world, but are instead using it as an instrument for their own political and ideological polemics and for their own psychological experience.

We also have the impression that there are those in areas of the press and publishing fields dealing with the third world who are thinking like this: The third world is just a timely subject through which one can carry on discussions about governments and the church. To them facts and the reality of the third world aren't of great importance; they are much more concerned about theories, hypotheses, and academic discussions. The great waste of ink and words, for instance, concerning the Latin American revolution! And for what? Instead of really helping the Latin Americans and other people understand their situation or helping them to make their own decisions in an autonomous way, the writers prefer simply to talk about the choices ("Others should decide, not we!") in a purely academic way, thus misinterpreting the meaning of our obligation to foster progress.

HOW TO SENSITIZE PUBLIC OPINION

What, then, is our real duty toward the third world? Here are three guidelines:

1. Progress is a product of justice and unity among all men. Therefore we must first understand this ourselves and then work to sensitize public opinion so that everyone in the Western world will realize his individual responsibility to contribute to the progress of humanity. When this happens, the pressure of public opinion will force governments to work for justice and disarmament, and to offer concrete, disinterested help to those who need it.

2. Peoples of the third world must be the creators of their own progress; we must help them in this respect by providing them with opportunities, with impetus, and the necessary assistance for their development.

3. The progress of people from both the third world and the Western world must be "integral." In other words, increased production and the promotion of social justice are not enough—we must not forget the spiritual and moral dimension of man either. Hence our duty toward the third world must be spiritual and Christian, not materialistic and agnostic.

Now let us not deceive ourselves; these convictions are far from being accepted by the majority of the peoples in the rich nations, who, as we have criticized before, have a sort of "beggar's mentality." This mentality is certainly not enough; we must make people understand that they must "pay personally," must renounce a part of their own welfare, in favor of our less fortunate brothers. More than ten years ago, P. Lebret wrote these words which are still valid today:

> The worst thing that exists in today's world is not the poverty of he who is deprived of means, but the lack of conscience of he who possesses them. Unfortunately, the Western world does not want to understand this, and it seems that it can't understand it. The Western world is imprisoned by its own old-fashioned conceptions, cultivating a mentality specifically colonistic, and maintaining itself by attaching to an economical system not up-to-date regarding the needs and the aspirations of the poor. The Western world, busy, above all, in keeping and increasing whatever it has, proves itself impotent to understand the world situation. The Western world does not see the necessity of a universal economy based on the need of the people, and the present form of communism believes in it even less. . . . The worst part is that the Western world has practically refused the scale of values that Christianity has brought to the world, the only real values that, as one can see today, could give life to a new civilization.[6]

In the last ten years Christians, at least, have not done enough to create a new mentality, despite the Council, the papal documents, the campaigns against hunger. Much has been done, but much more is left to be done. In order to be effective, the work of sensitizing the public to the needs of the poor nations must be carried on through every possible means (lectures, debates, articles, pamphlets, posters, and demonstrations) and must have the following essential characteristics:

(a) *Respect for the dignity of the people of the third world.* To show that such respect is not common, one need only turn back to the Campaign Against Hunger instituted in 1966, throughout many European countries to help India during its famine period. We heard then about the horrible aspects of hunger; we saw in the newspapers and on TV terrifying scenes that attempted to show the worst of the tragic situation. But there was nothing said to create an understanding of the Indians, nothing that would help Christians in the West to look upon the sufferers as brothers, or even to appreciate their ancient civilization. All we ended up with was a feeling of disgust for the Indian elite, looking upon their country as one of "death by starvation." And after Mrs. Indira Gandhi's justified attempts to defend her country's dignity, the resultant effect was the opposite of that which had been sought—many people began to react strongly against any kind of speech on hunger in the world.

This clearly demonstrates that, in order to carry on a public-opinion campaign for the third world, it is not enough simply to denounce hunger and injustice; we must start out with a sense of love and sympathy and understanding. We must not only want to impress, but to go deeper. No big headlines in the papers, but service to the poor. Finally, we should save the third world, not use it for our own benefits.

(b) *Respect for the culture of the third world.* Those who are really sincere in wanting to help the third world by collaborating with its peoples must have a thorough knowledge of the countries in question and the problems that hinder their progress. We cannot go on repeating the same things, the same statistics, the same slogans, and we cannot base our work on fleeting enthusiasms. This should be kept in mind by those movements organized to fight against hunger and poverty; otherwise, the organizations will lose their spirit and go on dealing with secondary subjects of momentary interest. Discussions about the underdevelopment of the third world should take place within the cultural framework outlined in the previous chapters, in order to reveal to our Western world the richness of the Afro-Asian and Latin American cultures and to make the West aware not only of what they can bring to these peoples, but what these peoples can bring to us. One cannot understand the differences between people if he only considers the political and economic aspects, because these, even if they are of more immediate interest, are much less deep than the social-cultural-religious ones; one cannot reach a point of understanding and collaboration without a dialogue concerning cultures and religions (or political ideologies). Therefore, in order to develop a profound and lasting interest, we believe that an in-depth study of the third world is of extreme importance.

(c) *Denunciation of injustice, but no provocation*. The campaign against hunger should not be conducted in a provocative way. Some of the participants may use the campaign as a means of protest, to make accusations against others, or for calling attention to all the other evils in the world. What they should be doing instead is convincing people, not provoking them; making them aware of poverty and injustice; and converting their minds and hearts, so that they too can see the misery that abounds and share our impulse to do something to eliminate it. It is not a question of "fight the others" (perhaps to prove that we have courage), but to inform and make others conscious of the wrongs we have discovered and which inspired in us fear and a desire to do something about them.

During a recent unsuccessful march against hunger, a group of young people, among whom were two priests, were carrying a vulgar and antiproductive sign: "When sh.. becomes of value, we will also take that away from the third world." Another group was shouting, "Down with the capitalists" and other such things. The reaction of even those who were in sympathy with the basic cause of the marchers was extremely negative, because they realized that the average person was bound to be offended by that kind of provocative behavior.

When you manage to disgust someone, you always create enemies for the cause for which you are fighting. Besides, it is childish to think that one can solve problems by shouting at everyone, and always to blame others. Work on behalf of the poor that is performed calmly and quietly, seems by far the best way to sway public opinion. Mother Teresa of India would seem a good example of this point.

Constructive criticism. The worth of any campaign against hunger can be judged, then, by asking oneself: Is it to help the poor, or is it also used as a motive to denounce the injustice of the wealthy? To repeat, injustice should certainly be denounced; but there are ways and ways to do it. It does not help to shout on the streets, "Down with the capitalists"—in fact, behavior of this sort only makes people lose faith in the campaign and in the ideas it wants to promote. In my opinion, the denunciation of injustice must be undertaken in a serious and concrete way and must be accompanied by proposed alternatives that are capable of becoming realities. To protest, or to suggest revolutionary hypotheses, without offering constructive proposals, can become mere verbal exercises, abstract and ambiguous.

Here are two instances that illustrate what we mean by concrete ways of fighting injustice:

In 1969, an election year in New Zealand, all Christian churches, youth groups, and movements working in behalf of the third world joined forces to initiate a new type of election campaign. It was not a question of getting members of any particular party to vote; instead, their slogan, "Let's send to Parliament men who will do something to fight hunger in the world," was addressed to the entire constituency. In planning the campaign the participants had prepared studies to prove to the public not only the fact of poverty in the third world, but also New Zealand's responsibility toward, and the advantages that it drew from, the poor nations' situation. There were, in addition, many lectures, discussions on national radio and TV, church sermons, and newspaper articles, all urging the public to vote only for those who would promise to take action against the injustice of which the third world was a victim.

That well-organized campaign was not without results. All the political parties became interested in the subject of the third world's development, and their nominees made it one of the main topics of their speeches, thus contributing to the awakening of the people's awareness of the problem. Additionally, the candidates for Parliament were forced to study the problem, and to commit themselves to helping to solve it.

All the responsible people of the various organizations who launched the campaign later stated that they had received formal assurances from the candidates and the political parties that their promises will be kept.

It is possible, of course, that many of the candidates will forget their promises, but at least they understand that their election had been conditioned by the problem of the fight against hunger, and this, in itself, is a great step forward.

The second instance was instigated by a foolish ambition to "denounce injustices"—but in this case the action was effective: Two years ago various movements for the third world that operate on the West Coast of the United States decided to experiment with the student movement of the local university, which was very active at that time in a students' protest. Together they made a serious study comparing New York banks with banks of other cities, in order to see where the banks' funds for foreign countries went. They found out that some banks were providing money for South Africa and Rhodesia, while others were not. So the students started a public-opinion campaign, accusing the banks under attack of favoring the state racism in southern Africa, and urging the public not to deal with them but to put their money into other banks which were not implicated in financing racist countries. There were silent "sit-ins" in front of some banks, articles in the newspapers, polemics, and marches against racism.

The ensuing scandal and the fact that the public was beginning to lose faith in their banks, prompted some stockholders to question the administrative boards as to whether it was worthwhile to maintain business relations with the racist countries. It was a full victory for the young people who started the movement of denunciation, for in a matter of a few months the accused banks published statements declaring that they would no longer finance the racist countries.

Other cases, with similar outcomes, have taken place like this in Anglo-Saxon countries; on the other hand, in the Latin countries we generally note foolish accusations which irritate people because they lack concrete value. It is useless to accuse capitalism in general. Let us document instead the real exploitation of some banks and some firms in regard to the third world and let us tell the public about it. The public will agree to join in taking action, and by means of one particular case will realize the existence of a much more general evil.

HELPING THE POOR TO BE THE SHAPERS OF THEIR OWN DEVELOPMENT

The second aspect of the obligation towards the third world is the *concrete help for the human growth of those populations*, so that they may start marching towards progress and have real opportunities. The underdevelopment of the third world derives, as we said, mostly from a lack of an inner impulse within static and conservative societies. There is also the aspect of international injustice when rich countries oppress and control the poor ones, but this is only one element that makes the country's situation worse—in fact, as we have said before, countries and peoples who were not colonized are the most underdeveloped and noncivilized. Therefore I don't think that international justice alone can solve the problem. Even if rich countries were perfectly fair towards the poor ones, the poor ones would still be underdeveloped (for the real causes are inside the country), and they would always need help. Even if the rich countries were to give them not one, but ten percent of their wealth, the poor countries—though they would, of course, have more money to spend—would still have the problem of underdevelopment. It is not true that with more money poor people would automatically be in better condition to develop themselves; too much money for one who does not know how to use it causes corruption and encourages wasteful spending. Look, in fact, at some very rich countries with petroleum "royalties," like Kuwait, Libya, Arabia, Iraq, and Iran; they are no better off than the poor countries which lack raw materials—such as Lebanon, Turkey, Tunisia, and Tanzania. That is why, as we have said, it is not money that creates the march for progress.

Justice among people is necessary, naturally; but it cannot play a solitary role in revising the drama of the setback of huge human masses. It needs the accompaniment of solidarity, brotherhood, and Christian charity that goes beyond the narrow concept of justice ("Justice is a minimum measure of charity," said Pius XII).

What can we do to help the countries of the third world begin their march for development and become themselves the creators of their own progress? We will not discuss here what the governments of the rich countries do, or the international organizations of the UN; this would take too long a time, as they are very complex. We already mentioned the importance of making the public aware of the problem so that it, in turn, will put pressure on the governments to act resolutely and generously in favor of the countries which are on the way to development. Besides, there is already in existence a vast amount of specialized literature[7] on what the governments should do, and we cannot present them in this little book, written only for the general public.

Therefore, we ask again: What must we do to really help the third world? Helder Camara, whom we mentioned before, used to say, "It would be absurd just to sit still, waiting for the governments to decide to move."

What we, organizations, unions, associations, and parishes can do is of extreme importance, since we have to assist people to become responsible for their own development with education, concrete help, and small ways that should serve as examples for them to imitate. And, as we have said, since underdevelopment is essentially a "failed development" of man, a failed set of conscience and mentality, a failed interior push of a culture towards modern progress, it is clear that the essential element for a people's development can only be in the formation of conscience and mentality; this is the push towards progress which can only come as a "revolution of ideas" about man, the world, and history. In a study of the Misereor,[8] one reads:

> The necessary arms to fight the underdevelopment are three: *first*, education, in order to change the mentality, to awaken the intelligence, to interest man in his future; *second*, cooperation, since man cannot develop by himself or change society by himself, but must work together with financial help and with technicians from outside, always helping and collaborating together; *third*, material help, to buy tools, to finance construction, and to create the necessary structures.[9]

A REVOLUTIONARY ACTION ON A POPULAR LEVEL

We must do something then for the third world or help the ones who are doing something already. The most important thing is to make the poor "aware of their poverty," according to the slogan used in Latin America by Helder Camara. Now, in order to educate the awareness of the poor, we must put ourselves absolutely on the same level as them, live with them, do social and educational work to change their mentality, and abolish the existing social structures, starting anew from a popular base. Missionaries and laymen, who leave their good countries and comfortable lives to go to places of poverty to live among people they don't know, in order to serve them, are the real "prophets" of international cooperation and of the fight against the world's hunger and injustice. If young people want to do something for the third world, they must forget themselves and give their lives (as missionaries) or, at least, give some years of their lives (as laymen). Cardinal Leger, who left Montreal to go to Cameroon to a leper hospital, wrote: "We talk a lot about the third world, but we prefer to live in our rich, developed world; it's more comfortable."

To leave his country and to give himself is the maximum proof and the maximum contribution that any young person can make toward helping the underdeveloped world.

We will not discuss here what should be done by missionaries and laymen for the third world, except to say that, in all the rich nations, very little has been done about it. And yet, there are a great number of young people everywhere who want to serve the third world. The missionary press and the missionary institutes know this well because every day they receive letters and visits from young people who want to engage themselves in the cause. I am sure not all the requests are expressions of real vocations to the service—sometimes it is only a desire to get away. But it would be wise to look into talents of these youths, who are eager to make their contributions to the progress of peoples.

What do missionaries, technicians, and laymen do in the third world to help people become the authors of their own development? They do revolutionary work at the popular level with schools, basic education and "micro-realizations." The funds for these social activities can come from anybody and depend totally on private donors and rich countries which are fighting against hunger.

The micro-realizations, small inexpensive projects, are easy to understand and to imitate. They serve as "models of development" for the entire region. A cooperative society of farmers, a model farm, a professional school, a radio for "basic education," the digging of a well or of a canal for irrigation, are all micro-realizations, which aid a village or a series of villages. One has to travel in the third world to realize how very effective these small things are and how they encourage people to work in order to become "executors of their own development."

I agree it is not with ten or with one hundred "micros" that you solve the problem of the setback of entire continents; however, this is better than staying comfortably seated at a table. Besides, the micro does not expect to solve all the problems; it is only a testimony, a sign of an awakening for the local population; it is a necessary work of "forming consciences" to enable the third world to begin marching forward. This system of the micro, given only to private organizations (generally Christian missions) is widely spread and used by the great organizations in the fight against hunger (Misereor, Oxfam, etc.). Oxfam began to finance the governments of the third world, but then, after years of experience, decided to finance only the projects of the local Christian churches. We must note that the micros are beginning to be unified in global projects for an entire country or territory.

Even the governments of the third world appreciate the micro system and have often invited local churches and other private organizations, which work in the field of development, to unify and program the initiatives. For instance, in March 1966, the AFPRO (Action for Food Production) was founded in India. It has two co-presidents, a Catholic and a Protestant, and coordinates all the social works of the Christian churches in India. In the first three years of activity, the AFPRO had dug something like thirty thousand wells, founded or financed hundreds of cooperatives, and set up courses in agriculture, mechanics, etc. Last year the Indian Minister of Agriculture, awarding a prize to the executives of AFPRO, said, "The work you have done, with so many well-coordinated little projects that you have completed with competence, is a strong push to improve agriculture and to improve life in the rural zones of our country. The Indian government is aware of what the private organizations can do in our country."

The necessity of the micro is also recognized by governments, since now everyone who dedicates himself to the progress of the third world knows that development will not be possible unless it operates from a low popular level: we must change men and mentality by trying to change the structures; if we change the structures from the outside, while local people are not prepared for changes, situations would become worse than before. The true revolution of the third world should not come about through little revolutionary groups of the elite, which impose their solutions on the people, but by the people themselves who, when they become aware of their dignity and rights, will wake from their present state of passivity and fatalism. The humble, unpublicized work of missionaries, sisters, and volunteer laymen, who live at the people's level and help them grow gradually, is the most revolutionary work that one can think of. Only in this way will we create the premises for the real march towards development and for all the social-political choices that this offers—choices which must be made by aware people and not by those who expect to take the people's place.

WHAT REALLY COUNTS: CREATING AN AWARENESS OF THE POOR PEOPLE

A last observation—F. Perroux writes:

> We have never seen in the history of the Western world, a class or a country which will give up its comforts to help a group which is less favored. Such real altruism, so exceptional among individuals, can never be found in organized groups.[10]

Many who believe it is necessary to be revolutionary to obtain international justice think like "good Christians" of the last century. They thought that by crying out against injustice and by engaging in "provocative" demonstrations, they would at last persuade the rich to be fair towards the poor. Finally, they made moralistic speeches against the "bosses": Be fair towards the workers. Be generous. This is exactly what those today are repeating: Justice for the poor people of third world. But in the Western world, justice became a fact when the workers, aware of their rights and of their human dignity, united and increased their "contractural" power. Therefore it was not the generosity of the bosses but the awareness of the workers that shifted the balance in favor of justice.

Now, how can we obtain international justice? By converting the rich or pricking their consciences concerning the poor? By praying that the rich will spontaneously renounce certain forms of exploitation? This is a delusion. We certainly must work to engender a social conscience in wealthy people, but we must first of all create an awareness in the poor, and raise them up so that they may start on their way. If we do this, "international justice" will come about naturally from their "contractual strength." Now to give people an awareness, we must absolutely engage in social and educational work at their level: and here is the value of the "micro," the value of going to the third world and putting ourselves at their service.

Certainly let us not scorn any attempts at making rich people aware of the injustice in the world and the misery of the poor; on the contrary, both rich and poor should be aware of these facts, if we want to bring about a "spiritual-Christian" view of development. But it is also true that if the poor people do not increase their "contractual strength" the rich will never act spontaneously in accordance with justice.

For instance, let us look at the communist countries which talk so much about justice; they take advantage of the third world as much as the capitalist countries do, paying cheaply for their raw materials, using political and financial blackmail, distributing their help in consideration for political power, etc.

What really counts is to help the countries of the third world change from a "static" to a "dynamic" period in their history, especially through popular education; after that, they will think of what to do and what to obtain for their development.

Sometimes we have the impression that certain "revolutionaries" want to make "political" speeches which mainly concern Western society, not the third world. This is only a cover-up for action based on our own situations, on the "third world in the West," and this means to take advantage of the third world, not help it. We, the organized movements for the fight against hunger, especially have to be on guard against these tendencies, which would destroy the ideals for which we stand, for the movements, born and affirmed by public opinion as organizations for the third world, may sometimes become attracted by the easy and snobbish game of global "disputes" with the excuse that, when the Western situation is changed, the third world also will benefit from it! Meanwhile we have speeches, meetings, and pamphleteering that have almost nothing to do with the third world except to provide an excuse for decrying "capitalism" (without mentioning the capitalism of communist countries) and everything adds up to words and discussions in a reminiscent style of the Jacobins, ready to start a new revolution.

We regret being a bit cynical about the young people, who, though animated by the best of intentions, are unable to choose the right ways to really help the third world's people. It often seems that some of these groups are desirous only of overthrowing the government or of dialoguing with the Marxists about global revolution, instead of being moved by compassion to give really concrete assistance to the poor of the third world. But—as Domenach wrote in

Esprit—"These are the times when a tendency toward irrationality makes the movement of the Left sterile."

Unfortunately, even some active groups against hunger in the world are contaminated by the leprosy of irrationality, building castles in the air, and wasting time on illusory schemes that are all out of proportion to their capabilities. A movement against hunger is not called upon to solve all the problems of humanity or to make any political choices for the third world. It should do what it can, generously and concretely, without believing that by just raising a big smoke, one can do much more. One must know his own limits.

FOOTNOTES

1. *See* "Il Giappone smentisce tutti i luoghi comuni sullo sviluppo," in *Mundo e Missione*, April 1970, pp. 226-228.

2. Dumont-Rosier, *La prossima crestia mondiale*, Jaca Book, Milan, 1967, pp. 219 ff.

3. The "green revolution" is the name given to the project aimed at increasing a country's food production within a short period through the introduction of a selected variety of seeds, artificial irrigation, chemical fertilizers, and new methods of cultivation. Above all, the "revolution" is due to Professor Borlany's discovery of new kinds of grains which yield two, three, or even four times as much as before. The most sensational results of the "green revolution" are to be seen in recent years in Pakistan and in India, two countries that were seemingly condemned to chronic famine.

4. The original title of the Pearson Report was *Partners in Development—Report of the Commission on International Development*, Praeger, New York, 1969.

5. E. Toaldo, "Helder Camara si spiega," in *Mondo e Missione*, November 1969, p. 518.

6. *Suicide ou survie de l'Occident?* Editions Ouvières, Paris, 1958, pp. 364-366.

7. In order to talk about what the governments and various organizations should do for the development of the third world, we should start by summarizing the already mentioned "Pearson Report," whose recommendations to rich countries (recommendations fully explained in hundreds of pages) are as follows: 1) establish a fair system of commercial exchange; 2) help investments in poor countries of private foreign capital; 3) increase the help given by governments, without attaching any political conditions; 4) solve the problem of debts incurred by poor countries as a result of loans by rich countries as these debts become an unbearable burden; 5) increase the help given by the International Organizations of the U.N.; 6) revise all the systems of help and technical assistance which could be more effective; 7) endeavor to establish birth control in poor countries.

8. Misereor is a German Catholic association expressly dedicated to contributing funds to development projects in the third world.

9. Cited in P. Vicentin, *Molti protestano, la "Misereor" aiuta*, in *Monde e Missione*, 1970, pp. 325-327.

10. In *La Croix*, Paris, April 22, 1967, p. 5.

CHRISTIAN OBLIGATIONS FOR A NEW WORLD

6

Christianity, which is interested in the development of the third world, often manifests a strange inferority complex. Christians wander in search of a message of liberation, without looking for the inspiration under their own roof, where they would find it very easily if they would only learn how to read the Gospel and the holy scriptures. Faced with hungry people and the inhuman misery that cries out for help, we uncritically follow Marxist theories, falsely revolutionary, without realizing that the biggest, most explosive revolution of history has its foundations in the word and example of Christ. Croce himself wrote: "Christianity is the greatest revolution that humanity has ever seen." Even for the most convinced Christians, Christ will always be the great unknown.

WHY SHOULD WE ACT AS CHRISTIANS?

In this last chapter we will examine the Christian's obligation toward the poor of the third world, that is, how he must act as a Christian. We are convinced, not only on the basis of faith but also on the basis of history, that Christ's message is the only one that can totally free man. In other words, the true liberation of man will come only from Christ. Some may regard this as blind faith. On the contrary, it indicates a trust in the human, as opposed to the divine, model that Christ has set before us—a trust that up to now has never been equalled in the history of man.

Nicolas Berdiaev wrote: "Even if Christ were not God, it would still be worthwhile to imitate Him."

It is well known that most movements against hunger and the movements for development of the third world started in Italy and in other countries with a fundamentally Christian culture (movements like: Mani Tese, Friends of the Lepers, Peace and Development, etc.). Now the young people involved in the movements often question the value of the Christian inspiration and are almost ashamed to act out of clear evangelistic inspiration. They claim that the "campaign against hunger" is a human action, not a religious one. And they are right. Not only Christians, but everyone, should be called to this work and everyone can work together for the same purpose of freeing man from need and oppression. It is true that a Christian must collaborate with anyone for the welfare of humanity. But it is equally true that a Christian of firm convictions must carry into his work spiritual and moral values that grow out of a well-defined Christian point of view. Christian inspiration has no meaning if someone merely wants to collect money to finance the construction of a technical school in the third world; it is best when each one contributes for his own personal reasons: out of a simple humanitarian motive, out of love for God, to aid in the struggle against imperialism, and so on.

But if the work we have to do is of a different kind, that is, if we have to sensitize public opinion, if we have to study the problems of the third world and the proposal of an integral model of development, then such a work cannot proceed without a clear "ideological" inspiration and without an integral model of a man to refer to.[1]

As the Development of Peoples says, "*All social action involves a doctrine*" (n. 39). This is natural. Every socio-political movement is striving for development, not underdevelopment. But each one wants a particular type of development that accords with its own vision of man, and often this conflicts with other types of development, as we have shown in the first part of this study. Development of a capitalistic or Marxist type is not like the Christian one.

Even the fight against hunger becomes a political action if it does not accomplish an effective work of collecting money; such an action cannot be regarded apart from "ideological" inspiration. In an excellent study on "Christian Anthropology and Political Duty" we read:

> Christians know that politics and religion are separate: but they also know that they cannot exist totally independent of each other. Some believe that political work should be performed separately. Religion should be a personal, private issue; political work should be based on worldly values proper to human beings. This position, which would reduce personality to schizophrenia, is not acceptable. Christians should work as Christians. For this reason they work not only for worldly values, but also to assure such conditions that will allow moral and religious life to subsist. Not accepting any middle-class, socialist, technocratic anthropologies, a Christian will start working politically to insert, partially and temporarily, his grain of "salt" within society: not the "salt" of wealth, of efficiency, of welfare, of productivity; but the "salt" of human dignity and the supernatural destiny of man.[2]

THERE IS NO TRUE HUMANISM WITHOUT CHRIST

The Christian, of course, knows that he is not superior to others, that he does not have a prepared solution for any problem. This is not all—he knows very well that development is a work of all men of goodwill, does not at all think that he is the only one concerned, and is ready to work with anyone for purposes and with means that do not conflict with his vision of man. He also knows that there are certain types of progress of materialistic inspiration which he cannot accept: for instance, capitalist-liberal progress, Marxist-communist progress, racist progress. A Christian must therefore work for human redemption of all men, animated by a Christian vision of the integral development "of all man and of all men," which has Christ as a model, for we believe that Christ is really the "new man," "the key, the center, the purpose of all human history."

We agree that the organizations for help and study of the third world are not instruments for "evangelization." They should not, and do not, depend on ecclesiastic hierarchies; these organizations should be made up of laymen and directed by laymen, with defined purposes in the human field, not in the ecclesiastic field. However, they should be Christian organizations, founded by Christians and with Christian purposes—that is, serving as witnesses to Christ, and not to be confused with evangelization, just as Christian inspiration is not to be confused with "confessionalism." All this because, for a true Christian, there is no true salvation or true humanism outside of Christ.

Therefore we do not bring impersonalized "values" to the third world, we do not bring an anonymous justice (different for each individual), but justice that mirrors God's justice. We do not bring solidarity simply as a human value but as charity taught and practiced by Christ. We do not bring a peace that excludes only war or is a result of the balance of power, but the peace of he who first said, "Peace be with you." This peace means, above all, no hate, no violence in man's heart.

In his Christmas address of 1969, Paul VI has made clear the difference between generic humanism and humanism according to the model of Christ. Here is a part of that interesting speech:

> Today the world talks about humanism. This is the modern term on which they base Christianity. They would like to celebrate the Christmas of man, not the Christmas of God who became flesh and of Jesus Savior, teacher and brother; they would like to celebrate the Christmas of man, who saves himself, who progresses with knowledge and power, who is the beginning and the end by himself.
>
> Here is what we have to tell you, sons and brothers, on this happy day: "A true humanism does not exist without Christ"; we beg God and all you men of the present, to avoid the fatal experience of a humanism without God.
>
> A consideration of yesterday and today's history should be sufficient to convince ourselves that human virtues without Christian faith may degenerate into vices, which are in contrast with them. The man who builds himself to be a giant, without a spiritual, Christian motive, falls because of his own weight, and lacks the moral strength that makes him a real man, lacks the capacity to judge the scale of values, lacks the transcendent reasons which should establish his motives and support his virtues; lacks a true knowledge of himself, of life, of the "whys" of history.
>
> By himself man does not even know who he is. He lacks the authentic prototype of humanity: he creates weak and sometimes vile idols. He lacks knowledge of the true Son of Man,

Son of God, the ideal model for the true man. Real humanism must be Christian as our first duty, our supreme concern.

What hope of real and constructive innovation could be given to you, young people, without the sure and always living word of him who, born for the world, can say: "Here, everything has been done anew"?

What freedom from oppression of fatigue and of social class differences will be offered to the labor world, which is seeking it in the changing of economic systems, if the voice of Christ does not raise it to the human, spiritual superior level? Remember, man does not live on bread alone.

And you, learned and patient creators of peace among people, among social classes, among racial and tribal conflicts, among wars of every kind, which often make men greedy, egotistical, and cruel, where will you find the energy to last in your long, beneficial work, if someone does not assist you; someone who can say with triumphal certainty: "Mind, men, you are all brothers."

LOVE ALONE IS REVOLUTIONARY

We now come to a consideration of the concrete applications of the Christian commitment to the third world. How are we to commit ourselves in accordance with the inspiration given by Christ, in accordance with Christ's model?

It seems to me the first point is this: at the basis of any action on behalf of the poor and the third world, we need love, an authentic spirit of universal charity.

"Justice without love," wrote Father Régamey, a Dominican who wrote a great deal on the theme of the poor, "is bitter and hard. We see too many Christians serving the cause of the poor with an unhealthy sourness in which hatred for the rich is more obvious than the evangelical spirit." We think that this spirit is largely derived from the Marxist principle of class struggle: Don Girardi states—in one of his short works[3]—that a Christian can accept the class struggle, provided he runs from any kind of violence and class hatred. This may be true in theory; but in practice, if a person joins in the dynamic of the class struggle, seen theoretically as the only means of liberating man, it is very hard for him to succeed in avoiding hatred. Moreover, it is well known that hatred of the "enemies of the proletariat" is a basic element in communism. Lenin praised comrade Gallacher because he was "animated by a noble proletarian hatred . . . . This hatred is truly the beginning of all wisdom, the foundation of every socialist and communist movement and one of its victories."[4]

The constant teaching of all Soviet pedagogy is to "educate people in hatred of the enemies of the people and the socialist state." The classic interpreter of Soviet pedagogy, Makarenko, says that "class hatred must spring from an inner revulsion toward the enemy."[5]

Khrushchev said, "If there is the revolutionary spirit in you . . . if there is in you the spark of hatred for the enemy, take up the banner of Marxism-Leninism. Hatred of the class enemy is necessary because you cannot become a good fighter for communism if you are not capable of hating the enemy."[6]

The communist theoretician, Kuusinen, wrote:

> Whoever attenuates class conflicts, proposes to suspend the struggle of the worker classes, commits himself to soften and weaken it, and preaches social peace, is in substance . . . an enemy of progress, and a promoter of stagnation and regression. Such a position is unacceptable for the workers and for all progressive men.[7]

We also find the same basic position with the latest revolutionaries who are inspired by communism. For example, in a letter in 1967, shortly before he died, Che Guevara wrote:

> *Hatred is an important factor of the struggle:* an implacable hatred of the enemy, a hatred that spurs man on to overcome his natural limitations and makes him an effective machine for killing, a machine both vigorous and cold. Our militants must be like this; a people without hatred is incapable of conquering a brutal enemy.[8]

We have insisted on this point because it seems to us that it is not infrequent to see the case of young Christians who, starting out with the desire to serve the third world, let themselves become fascinated by the dynamic of the "class struggle," and the hatred of the "enemies of the people": The third world then becomes nothing else but a pretext for following aberrant dreams of more or less global revolution, nurtured on bitterness, rage, pessimism, and violence. All of this, we are convinced, represents the suffocation of any concrete realization of a better mankind: "Hatred does nothing but destroy; only love builds" (Abbé Pierre).

Another great liberator of the poor, Martin Luther King, thought along the same lines:

> Among us there are hard-hearted and bitter individuals who want to fight their opponents with physical violence and corrosive hatred. *Violence only brings temporary victories;* in creating more problems than it solves, it never brings permanent peace. I am convinced that if we yield to the temptation to use violence, future generations will have to suffer a long and desolate night of bitterness, and our chief legacy to them will be an interminable reign of chaos.
>
> Why should we love our enemies? The first reason is quite obvious: returning hatred for hatred multiplies hatred, adding deeper darkness to a starless night. Darkness cannot dispel darkness; only the light can do this. Hatred cannot dispel hatred; only love can. Hatred multiplies hatred, violence multiplies violence, hardness multiplies hardness, in a descending spiral of destruction.
>
> Another reason is that hatred disfigures the soul and disturbs the personality; it is harmful to the personality of one who hates. Like a cancer, hatred corrodes the personality and devours its vital union. Hatred destroys in a man his sense of values and objectivity; it brings him to describe the beautiful as ugly and the ugly as beautiful, to confuse the true with the false and the false with the true.
>
> A third reason why we should love our enemies is that love is the only force capable of transforming an enemy into a friend. We will never free ourselves from an enemy by responding to hate with hate; we free ourselves from an enemy by liberating ourselves from enmity. *By its very nature hatred destroys and wounds; by its very nature love creates and builds.*
>
> We must hasten to say that these are not the definitive reasons why we must love our enemies. One even more fundamental reason is expressed explicitly in Jesus' words: "Love your enemies . . . so that you may be sons of your Father who is in heaven." We are called to this difficult task with the purpose of establishing a unique relationship with God. We are potentially sons of God; through love, this potentiality becomes actual. We must love our enemies because only by loving them can we know God and experience the beauty of his holiness.[9]

THE REAL REVOLUTION: THE REVOLUTION OF CONSCIENCES

The second characteristic of the Christian commitment to the development of peoples is the rejection of violence, of violent revolution as a privileged means for man's liberation. The word "revolution" is understood not in a univocal way. Christians too want revolution, i.e., the radical change of the political, social, and economic organization, with the abolishment of all the present injustices and inequalities that divide men, social classes, and peoples. But the Christian is convinced that *the real revolution is above all the revolution of consciences*, which enters thoroughly into man and transforms him. Then man can gradually transform the society in which he lives. A revolution from the outside, imposed with violence, remains ineffective if men are not prepared to build a new society.

Here we shall return to the discussion opened in the first chapter of this volume, when we were pointing out the diversities that exist between a Christian notion and a Marxist (or capitalist) notion of development.

The Christian (or the person who is "spiritual"-minded) is convinced that the real prime mover of development is man, and therefore in order to transform the structures of society for the better, *man himself must first of all be transformed* in his conscience, his mentality, his vision of the world and history, and be convinced that he has to renounce his own selfishness, at least to some extent. Naturally there must also be some action on the political level—influence over the structures themselves, a direct action aimed at transforming the laws, lifestyles and organization of society. But this action will only be effective when it is sustained freely and with innermost conviction by the majority of a political community and as the consequence of a better formation and human maturity. A revolution imposed by force and by an elite minority is never successful. The minority may indeed win power, but then it has to keep it by force. *The structures change, but the old law that regulates the world remains: the law of the strongest.*

This is not a true revolution but simply a change in the men in power, who merely change the norms of man's dominance over man. I was able to witness this in the summer of 1970 in Cuba[10] where Castro's revolution had idealized force and violence and where the "dictatorship *of* the people" was transformed into a "dictatorship *over* the people." In Cuba, whoever does not accept the structures imposed by the new regime, whoever does not agree with Marxism-Leninism, is marginalized from society, looked upon as suspect and mauled by the imposing apparatus of the military police. And this is exactly what had happened in the previous regimes. Previously Batista and the capitalists were in command. Today it is Castro and the communists, and a new "caste" of "revolutionaries" has taken power. But the Cuban people have changed very little: the individual has no value, his rights are oppressed. In some areas (education, health) his existence may have improved, but in others it has worsened (very strict police control, and ideological discrimination in society, etc., are sources of new injustices that are no less grave than the previous ones).

For me the case of Cuba has been an exemplary lesson. Violence, hatred, the struggle "on principle" against others, the notion of development as something to be imposed by force on all the people, do not lead to peace, authentic progress, or justice. It is not enough to change unjust structures. We must change the rules of human society. We must change man. And man does not change in depth unless there is love, and respect for others, for their ideas, for their freedom and rights. All this requires time and in-depth training; man does not change in the way structures of society do, overnight.

Péguy wrote: "*Social revolution will be moral or it simply will not be.*" We can paraphrase this by saying that with hate, compulsion, violence, and contempt for man, at the most we can destroy, but we can construct nothing positive. An authentic revolution can be made only with love.

VIOLENT REVOLUTION IN LATIN AMERICA?

Must we therefore exclude, in every case and absolutely, the use of violence in order to modify the unjust structures of a given society? The problem is difficult to resolve and even Christian theologians have not yet given a common and definite answer. We cannot delay then over the various positions, but it seems to me that we can agree with René Coste, a specialist in international morality:

> From a Christian point of view we cannot exclude every hypothesis of recourse to violence. The evangelical commandment

of nonviolence is not the supreme commandment. The only supreme commandment is that of charity, love expressed through concrete actions. Now, the fulfillment of this commandment is left to our responsibility as men. The Gospel offers us a basic orientation and not recipes or, even less, a code of ethics. Each Christian, when the actions of nonviolence have run dry or else have been discarded because they were ineffective, can on his own personal responsibility decide whether recourse to violence has to be taken out of love for his brothers in order to defend them effectively against an unjust aggressor, although he knows that this is only an emergency measure.[11]

As it is not possible to condemn in the absolute every defensive war (as in the case of the war and the resistance against nazism and fascism), it is also not possible to condemn in the absolute every revolt against an unjust oppressor, once peaceful solutions in both cases have been tried and failed. Judgments in concrete cases no longer involve theology, but rather political analysis. At the end of a long study, Father Ernesto Toaldo writes:

The question that arises is whether a revolutionary war is necessary and politically useful in a given country and in particular circumstances when there is a politico-economic authority that oppresses citizens, and thereby has already taken the initiative in the use of violence. . . . If it is demonstrated that a revolutionary war is the only means for obtaining justice in the given situation, then, from a personal point of view, such a revolutionary war is even morally justifiable. But it cannot be claimed that the Church and all Christians think in this way. Everyone must behave in accordance with the kind of political judgment that he himself has made of the situation. We must therefore allow here, as in other political problems, the fullest scope o' opinions: a respectable pluralism. . . . In each case, the Christia must remember that violence as such is not a value, but merely a lesser evil and therefore may be contested before, during, and after the revolution as well. "Violence," René Coste emphasizes, "must be contested at the very time of its being exerted, because it has no value in itself. Let us seek not to transfer to revolutionary violence the so-called values that were once attributed to war." Even if we understand Che Guevara's anger in his *Message to the Peoples of the World*, the Christian must reject a struggle to the death without any moral norm, such as Che conceives it. Nor can a Christian accept the norm formulated by Marcuse, according to which "every revolution builds its own moral norms. . . ." *A Christian must avoid making an idol out of a (violent) revolution, and consecrating it as an Absolute.* On the contrary, he must relativize it in view of the supreme values, God, and man.[12]

Today the problem of revolutionary violence is presented in a special way by Latin America. In this regard, the Most Reverend Marcos MacGrath, Archbishop of Panamá, vice-president of CELAM, and an expert on the problems of development, writes:

> The thought of so many Europeans and North Americans on the theme of revolution and the rapid change of structures in Latin America arises out of other mental categories. It never focuses on the fact that the starting point for development is above all awakening the awareness and consciences of the poor. Basically there is the error of thinking of development as something imposed from the outside, whether with violent or nonviolent means. I do not agree with the many people who speak of the need for recourse to violence in Latin America: above all because of the generality of these statements and then also because no prudent judgment can be formulated in the abstract; it has to consider the situation of the particular place. Choosing violence is a very grave decision: in every case people take a local and personal position. The Church's task is to give the principles, and thereafter each person is called upon in conscience to act; if some, in a particular situation of hopeless injustice, choose this route, I hope they are well enough informed Christians that they can arrive at a choice that has been meditated upon and thought through. . . . However, I am convinced that we must follow the line of a tenacious mobilization and formation of the consciences of Christians on all levels. We shall then arrive at the creation of grass-roots groups, cooperatives, and unions that then can bring the necessary pressures to bear on their own leaders for the necessary changes."[13]

What we Christians challenge is the concept that struggle and violence are the privileged means for the liberation of man. Yet it is a very widespread concept of Marxist and communist origin: *Underdevelopment is reduced to an oppression of the rich in their dealings with the poor and development is conceived as a struggle against the rich of the world.* This manner of schematizing an extremely complex problem does not seem right to us, i.e., it does not seem to correspond with the reality of the facts. Development is above all the formation of man, the building of more just societies, the creation of wealth by means of common labor, and the overcoming of mentalities and traditions that stand in the way of progress.

No one denies that between the rich peoples and the poor there are injustices and oppressions that call for political and trade-union action against every kind of exploitation, both on the national and international levels. But to reduce the whole problem of poverty in the world to the dynamic of exploitation and the struggle between the rich and the poor is not only false but counterproductive for the poor countries of the third world themselves.

As previously mentioned in Chapter Four, *Esprit* editor J. M. Domenach criticizes as deeply irrational Claude Julien's book *America's Empire*, in which the author states that the countries of the third world are poor because they are exploited by American imperialism and concludes by saying that the wealth of America is a pie made from the exploitation of other peoples; therefore it is necessary, even by violence, to slice up this pie. Domenach, addressing himself to this point, writes:

> This pie does not exist: the economic wealth of the world is made up above all of an ensemble of forces that inter-react by helping and hindering one another: labor, resources, technology, population, transportation, money, etc. It is not a warehouse, a granary, or a pie. To allow this to be believed is to encourage the underdeveloped peoples to build up illusions that will turn against them and accentuate their dependence in their confrontations with the great industrial powers, which know that prosperity is not a pie to be divided but wealth to be built up.[14]

For a Christian, development arises not only out of a struggle against others—even though in certain cases it may be necessary to fight—but from collaboration with others; not from the class struggle but from collaboration among the social classes; not from the struggle between rich and poor peoples but from aid and collaboration on a world scale; not from war and the law of the strongest, but from peace in justice and brotherhood.

CONTESTING CAPITALIST SOCIETY

Certainly, we are perfectly aware that it it is not enough to preach justice, peace, brotherhood, and collaboration. It is also necessary to protest against the injustices in the world and to make society evolve towards organizational forms that are less inhuman. The Council stigmatized mankind's present situation:

> . . . we are at a moment in history when the development of economic life could diminish social inequalities if that development were guided and coordinated in a reasonable and human way. Yet all too often it serves only to intensify the inequalities. In some places it even results in a decline in the social status of the weak and in contempt for the poor.
>
> While an enormous mass of people still lack the absolute necessities of life, some, even in less advanced countries, live sumptuously or squander wealth. Luxury and misery rub shoulders. . . . Hence, numerous reforms are needed at the socioeconomic level, along with universal changes in ideas and attitudes.[15]

If the Christian rejects Marxism and institutionalized violence as a solution to mankind's problems, he also rejects the present capitalistic organization of society; statements by Christians in this sense are very numerous, from the Council and papal encyclicals to the reflections of scholars and the pronouncements of certain groups and congresses. There is an embarrassment of choice. For example, in the papal letter to the 40th Week of Social Studies (Brescia, October 30–November 4, 1970) we find many indications of contestation with the present organization of society. Here is one:

> Man's dominion over the forces of nature is growing day by day. But it cannot always be said that the capacity for doing good with these forces is growing at the same rate as technological conquests. . . . We see the particularly dehumanizing effects of industrialized societies, which have as their motivation efficiency raised to the first criterion of evaluation and judgment; the preeminence accorded to consumption over other considerations of the human order; and the subordination of the person to the needs of the organization. The priority of efficiency has now become a myth; whoever does not operate in terms of profit is put on the fringes of society, isolated, and destroyed; the hegemony of consumption gives more power, attention, and esteem to the one who consumes more without reference to moral values; the supremacy of the organization, to the detriment of the person, is favored by automatized processes in the economy and in social life. Other major dangers which are incumbent on man today

because of the typical structures of industrialized society are the growing manipulation of man and the advent of a soulless society that would be capable of suffocating cultures and the highest expressions of the human spirit. . . . *Society no longer has man and his integral development as its goal.*

It is not a question of condemning technical progress and industrialization by proposing a utopian return to the living conditions of the pre-industrial period. On the contrary, the peoples of the third world themselves who are still living in that period are tending to come out of it in forced stages. *Often the production of wealth is confused with its distribution; it is the distribution that is unfair, not the fact of production itself.* But the joint development of all men implies a greater production of wealth in order that there be something for everyone. Liberation from enslavement to the most elementary needs (hunger, sickness, illiteracy, nakedness) is the first step towards man's total development, his "integral development."

We acknowledge, therefore, that technological progress and industrial organization are instruments that are good in themselves. But we must act, as Christians, to make sure that they are not used inhumanly, but rather in man's service and not in his oppression.

ECONOMY IN THE SERVICE OF MAN

Unfortunately, economy and modern society seem to have lost sight of the service of man. More than thirty years ago Einstein noted this: "Our age is characterized by a search for perfection in regard to means, but for confusion as regards the ends."

Today as never before the men and societies of the developed countries have been freed from material needs and have in their possession very powerful means for transforming the world and the human community. Indeed, it seems that peace, universal brotherhood, and the joint development of all men are on the verge of being achieved. There are now means for doing away with hunger, illiteracy, and all the other centuries-old plagues that oppress man. If these goals have not yet been reached, it is only because the majority of men and the societies that represent them are still unclear about the fact that material development is at the service of the whole human community; the means, the wealth, the industrial and technological power are there, but people as yet do not know how to make use of them. Modern society is not so much lacking in organization, structures, power, or wealth *as it is in spiritual and moral values*, which indicate the route to be taken for the welfare of all.

Thus the economy of the rich countries is directed to two finalities, both of which are contrary to man's advancement and the development of all men: *arms and waste*. Josué de Castro wrote:

> The economy of the rich countries is still a war economy. Everything is based on national defense. Now it is perfectly obvious that two things cannot be done at the same time: produce more armaments that are increasingly more numerous and costly, and help the underdeveloped world to progress. A choice must be made: *either a war economy or a peace economy*.[16]

When one thinks that throughout the world military expenditures now exceed 200 billion dollars a year, one cannot but agree that the Brazilian scholar is right: aid from the rich countries to the poor reaches only the 10-billion-dollar-mark per year, which is only 5 percent of the military expenditures! Truly a collective madness!

Another madness is the waste and the "consumer" trend of the population in industrial countries. The phenomenon has already been amply described and contested.[17] Modern industry, in part at least, is no longer working to satisfy man's authentic needs, but rather to create new ones which are in part superflous and to work to satisfy them. We therefore have a "waste economy" sustained by a kind of advertising that brutalizes and rapes the consumer, leaving him always still unsatisfied. Is it authentic progress to flood the market with ever-new kinds of detergents, beauty creams, automobiles, refrigerators, television sets, eccentric fashions, etc.? How many perfectly useless products have been foisted on consumers in the rich countries?

People will say this is the law of industrial production and progress. But they are wrong, since industry would advance of its own accord if, instead of producing useless or superfluous things, it would produce in order to meet the many essential needs of man that are still not met even in rich countries—think only of housing, education, health, public transportation, sports facilities for all, etc.

Let us note again that this mad rush into "consumerism" (in the derogatory sense of the term) is negative not only for the people of the rich countries themselves (pollution of the air, water, and soil; neuroses; intellectual apathy; poorer health), but it is also ruinous for the developing countries, where Western consumer-advertising is creating the same mechanisms as in our countries. Even in places where hunger and illiteracy still exist, we see the appearance of industries that turn out beauty products, detergents that wash "whiter than white," and other similar products. How can we blame the poor of the world, who are more defenseless than we in the face of the assault on "consumer" well-being, when at home our own poor skip meals or live in hovels so that they can buy a television set or the latest thing in clothes? When in the face of the misery in our own countries, we have special food for cats and dogs, buy a new car every two years, spend incredible sums to create products that are increasingly more sophisticated and superfluous? The famous adage "we must eat to live and not live to eat" is becoming less and less applicable; in the developed countries—as among the upper classes of the underdeveloped countries—it is getting truer and truer that *man lives to eat even when he is not hungry; lives to consume, to produce more and consume more.*

This waste of money, human energies, and natural resources is paid for by the poor of the world whose estrangement from the rich is becoming ever more abysmal, since the rich, instead of using their wealth to help their brothers in need, are pursuing an illusory materialistic happiness which they will never achieve. Abbé Pierre is right when he writes:

> The poor do not envy those more privileged than they. What the poor do not accept—and in their refusal they are God's witnesses—is *useless privilege*, the privileged person whose privilege becomes a robbery, even if it was acquired honestly, to the extent that *it is not useful in the service of the "little ones" and the suffering*. What the poor ask for and require is not the leveling-off of wealth; what they require is honesty, whereby if you have more you will serve more. Of the rich this is demanded: to be honest and to ask yourself every day: *Did I earn my privilege today?* [18]

Christians, the rich and privileged peoples, therefore have the duty not to accept the present situation in economy and human society, but to be committed to finding new and more human solutions. In the Pope's letter to the 57th Social week in France (Paris,

July 1-5, 1970), dedicated to the theme "The Poor in the Society of the Rich," we read:

> For Christians, it is not a question of committing their forces to the search for a utopian and egalitarian society. On the contrary, it is to protest with all their might, in the name of the Gospel, against the primacy of an economics that tends to legitimize a "residual" poverty as the tribute that must necessarily be paid for growth and development. If it were possible to say that wealth is a machine that makes the poor, it is necessary to denounce such an inhuman notion and to be committed with all one's might against this manifold egoism, by promoting an authentic and integral development, i.e., "of each man and each group of men" (Development of Peoples, n. 14). Such an endeavor will tend in the first place—is there need to emphasize this?—to prevent certain categories of persons, who are in various ways victims of economic growth, from being rejected and put on the fringes of society, to the point of constituting subhuman groups of people. . . .

The letter concludes on a note about the commitment of Christians:

> By rejecting the illusion of a lasting and beneficial change that would be assured by a violent upheaval, like the myth of an equilibrium progressively acquired solely by means of the free play of economic factors, you will be committing yourselves with sane realism to transforming the present structures little by little in order to eliminate that phenomenon which is constantly cropping up beyond ideologies, whereby the fruits of common labor are confiscated by an abusive minority. You will thus be building a society which will no longer be dominated by prestige, egoism, and profit, but will be concerned with sharing, giving and serving . . . "where each man will be loved and helped as his brother, as his neighbor" (Development of Peoples, n. 82).

The commitment of Christians—and all men of goodwill—is therefore along this line: that in society the service of the strongest to the weakest will prevail over profit and private or caste egoism. *The joint development of mankind is therefore a moral political problem even before it is an economic and technical one*, in the sense that it implies a radical revolution in the mentality and will of peoples and governments.

"On the one hand," writes Father Lebret, "the mentality of power and domination on the part of the rich has to be changed; on the other hand, the fatalistic and conformist mentality of the poor also has to be changed, with a mentality nurtured by a taste for progress and by the desire to arrive at complete development."

On one side, it is not enough to furnish underdeveloped peoples with capital, machines, and aid of various kinds. We must create in them the will for development, since progress is not a gift from the outside, but must arise out of the labor and organization of individual countries, out of a transformation of mentalities, structures, and traditions.

On the other side, the rich peoples must become aware that the poor will never succeed on their own in getting excited about development and in setting out with the sufficient rapidity demanded by demographic growth and the expectations of the masses. If we do not wish that the abyss between the rich and the poor of the world grow ever deeper, we must express a political will that will succeed in placing Western society on another line of march: not that of technological progress as an end in itself and selfishly preserved for itself, but of aid and brotherly service to the poor so that all may have humane life conditions.

This is the meaning of the Christian argument with present-day society; it is not merely negative but aimed at building *a new world that must rise out of the conquering of sefishness and materialism*, from the birth of new criteria of values and judgments. Today, the "hidden persuasion" of commercial advertising and the social communication media has succeeded in convincing man in the rich countries (and also in the poor countries as well) that the objects produced by man are essential in order for him to be happy. People take "things" very seriously and think that their happiness increases in proportion to their well-being and their possession of an ever-greater number of consumer goods, which at times they literally do not know how to consume or which are quite harmful to their physical or psychical equilibrium if they do consume them. Happiness and personal success are measured by the quantity of things possessed.

But each of us knows from daily experience that this is not the case. Social tensions, dissatisfaction, the protest of youth, even in richer societies and families, clearly demonstrate that *selfish enjoyment of ever-increasing prosperity is not the road that leads to happiness and peace.*

What alternative must the Christian offer and bear witness to in his life? *There is no doubt that this alternative is Christ;* he is not a sociologist, a politician or even a philosopher, but he proposed to man his own love even to the point of his sacrifice of himself, and he indicated in brotherly love the divine commandment. That is the luminous road which men must take if they want to get out of the blind alley into which selfishness has driven them and find happiness insofar as that is possible in the human condition.

How well Abbé Pierre writes when he synthesizes the whole Christian message: "My happiness is not in securing my own happiness but rather that of others."

FOOTNOTES

1. Highly recommended on this point is *Liberation, Development and Salvation* by Rene Laurentin (Orbis Books, Maryknoll, N.Y. 1972).
2. G. Morra, "Antropologia cristiana e impegno politico," in *Studi Cattolici*, Milan, November 1969, pp. 760-761.
3. *Cristianesimo e lotta di classe*, Centro di Documentazione, Pistoia, 1969.
4. Quoted in G. Lojacono, *Il Marxismo*, 3d ed., E. D. I., Naples, 1967, pp. 55-56.
5. *Ibid*.
6. N. Khrushchev, *I problemi della pace*, Einaudi, Turin, 1964, p. 123.
7. Kuusinen et al., *Principi elementari del Marxismo*, Vol. II, Editori Riuniti, Rome, 1962, p. 77.
8. The letter was addressed to the secretary of OSPAAL, Oberbaum Presse, Berlin, 1967. Quoted in "Justice dans le Monde," Louvain, September 1968, p. 13.
9. *The Strength to Love*, New York, Harper and Row, 1963, passim.
10. *See* P. Gheddo, "Un mese con la rivoluzione cubana," in *Mondo e Missione*, special service of February 1971.
11. "Violence et Révolution," in *Nouvelle Revue Théologique*, 1969, pp. 78 ff.
12. "Chiesa e rivoluzioni nel terzo mondo," in *Mondo e Missione*, special service of December 1970.
14. "L'Empire Américain," p. 642.
15. *The Church in the Modern World*, n. 63.
16. In *La Croix*, Paris, December 13, 1966, p. 3
17. *See* J. K. Galbraith, *The Affluent Society*, Rev. ed., New York, New American Library, Mentor Books, 1971; and G. Hourdin, *Les chrétiens contre la société de consommation*, Calman Levy, Paris, 1969.
18. Abbé Pierre, "Il cristiano di fronte ai poveri," in *Le Missioni Cattoliche*, Milan, March 1968, p. 133.

SUGGESTIONS FOR ACTION

The Bible is not only a book to read; it is also a way of life. If we attempt to live according to the Scriptures, we must realize that we are being called into action. The perspective of our action should be global. For we know that the implications of our inaction are global.

Most of us can do little by ourselves. Our first step should be to get in touch with others who are already involved in the world struggle for justice. There are hundreds of groups and organizations in the United States which focus on world affairs or international justice.

For a listing and description of over 200 such educational and action groups representing a variety of special concerns and a spectrum of political opinion, write for the special issue of *Intercom* (May-June 1969), entitled "U.S. Voluntary Organizations and World Affairs" ($1.50 from *Intercom*, Center for War/Peace Studies, 218 E. 18th Street, New York, N.Y. 10003). Some examples of the listings:

1. *National Council of the Churches of Christ in the U.S.A.*, 475 Riverside Dr., New York, N.Y. 10027, *Department of International Affairs:* Serves as a Christian witness concerning the positions of our nation and its government relative to international order, justice, freedom, and peace; undertakes programs of education and action, research and development, among clergy and laity, including nationwide

study and discussion programs on world affairs, international consultations, national conferences, seminar sessions for leaders at the Church Center for the UN; issues materials; audio-visual aids.

2. *United States Catholic Conference, Department of International Affairs, Division of World Justice and Peace*, 1312 Massachusetts Ave., N.W., Washington, D.C. 20005: Stimulates awareness among U.S. Catholics of their responsibility for promotion of world justice, development and peace. Creates a "conscience lobby" for the poor of the world; develops an awareness of and commitment to the urgent needs of the "third world"; recommends diocesan programs and seminars; promotes panel discussions, workshops, and study projects; issues discussion and program materials.

3. *Overseas Development Council*, 1717 Massachusetts Ave., N.W., Washington, D.C. 20036: Keeps tab on research being done on development including trade and foreign investment; determines additional needs and encourages and supports their fulfillment; disseminates information through publications, conferences, seminars, and liaison with other national organizations.

4. *American Freedom from Hunger Foundation*, 1717 H St., N.W., Rm. 437, Washington, D.C. 20006: Seeks to acquaint the American public with the problem of world hunger and the necessity for sending technical assistance to underdeveloped countries as part of worldwide Freedom from Hunger campaign; sponsors community youth mobilization program, "Walks for Development."